ARMED DEFENSE

GUNFIGHT SURVIVAL FOR THE HOUSEHOLDER AND BUSINESSMAN

ARMED DEFENSE

GUNFIGHT SURVIVAL FOR THE HOUSEHOLDER AND BUSINESSMAN

by
Burt Rapp

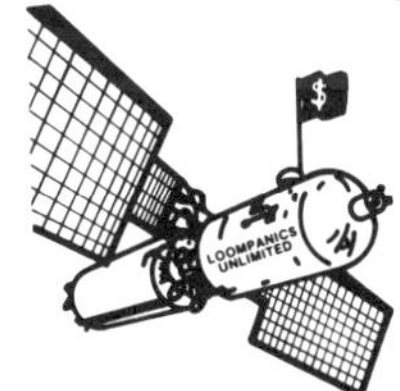

Loompanics Unlimited
Port Townsend, Washington

Neither the author nor the publisher assumes any responsibility for the use or misuse of information contained in this book. It is sold for entertainment purposes only. Be warned!

ARMED DEFENSE

Printed in the USA

Published by:
Loompanics Unlimited
PO Box 1197
Port Townsend, WA 98368

Illustrations by Shawn Ajax

ISBN 1-55950-014-X
Library of Congress Catalog Card Number 89-084029

THANKS

Many people, police officers and civilians, helped make this book possible. There are too many to list by name, but they know who they are. This is my thanks and sincere appreciation for the effort.

TABLE OF CONTENTS

INTRODUCTION

This book concerns defending yourself with a gun. Many people are buying guns for protection in response to the increasing crime rate. Gunhandling skill is another matter. Not all are equally proficient. How is your skill? Do you know how to load and fire your weapon? Are you a good shot? How about combat-style tactics? Do you know what to do to defend your life?

There have been lots of books and articles written dealing with defense against crime. Most give advice about locks and alarms. Some even advise the reader not to buy a gun because it could be more dangerous to himself than to the criminal. This defeatist viewpoint is typical of the person who knows nothing about guns.

This book is for the person who has decided to use a gun for protection. If you prefer to hand over your wallet to the thug, stop reading right here. If you feel that extra locks and alarms are all you need, don't read any more. If you truly feel that you could not use deadly force against a person threatening your life, this book is not for you. Make out your will and be sure your insurance is paid up.

This is a nuts-and-bolts book, with little academic discussion. We won't waste time on the big controversies such as "stopping power," the revolver vs. auto pistol debate, and other issues. Let's also not waste time philosophizing about causes of crime, capital punishment, and social problems.

Instead, we'll study practical defense against dangerous criminals. We'll study active and passive tactics, types of weapons to use, and how to gain the edge over the thug.

The intruder or hold-up artist has the edge if you're unprepared, but if you stack the odds in your favor you can win. This book is for the significant majority of honest citizens who don't wish to be robbed, burglarized, or raped.

The criminal is the aggressor, and in principle the aggressor has the tactical advantage. However, most street thugs are bullies at heart. They don't expect resistance, and anyone who resists gains surprise over the criminals.

Armed resistance is also a deterrent. The criminal who knows the householder is armed will hesitate. In fact, states which have few or no gun control laws have few break-ins while the citizens are home. By contrast, in places such as New York City, where it's a felony for a citizen to own an unlicensed gun, criminals crash in every day.

The aim of this book is to provide you with some basic building blocks of tactics to use if ever you face a show-down. There's no absolute prescription for every situation, and no tactical plan that will cover every case. Instead, the approach will be to lay out the basics, so that you can build your own plan to suit the situation when it occurs.

This book will show you how to teach yourself to shoot well enough to save your life in a variety of situations. You'll learn techniques and tactics that work, not just reflections of somebody's theories. You'll find out how to protect yourself by deciding what tactics you need. This book will also cover what you need to know about the legal and emotional aspects of surviving a gunfight.

THE ODDS AGAINST YOU

Before deciding about a gun, you ought to know what your chances are. A few statistics can help.

We've heard the statement: "The cops are never there when you need them." According to Lieutenant Norman Cook, of the Phoenix, Arizona, Police Department, almost 20% of the calls to the police emergency number are put on "hold" for 10 to 40 seconds. If you get put on "hold," you're in serious trouble. It's the same in many other cities. You're on your own. The police won't defend you against crime. They'll show up after it's all over and take a report.

Can the police even defend themselves? Not always. Dozens are shot in the line of duty every year.

What about your odds of surviving an armed encounter with a criminal? Some would have you believe that you're better off unarmed because you'll shoot either yourself or a member of your family. The facts don't support this viewpoint. A study of a collection of newspaper clippings dealing with criminal incidents reveal the following statistics: there were 40 attackers and a total of 50 defenders. Eight defenders were armed with pistols. Attackers were armed in 22 incidents, 15 with handguns, 3 with knives, and 4 with clubs.

Seventeen defenders were killed, and all were unarmed. There were only 2 exchanges of shots. One defender, a storekeeper, was mistakenly killed by police who interrupted a crime in progress. Twenty of the criminals escaped. Three were wounded, 1 captured, and 1 killed himself.

Although this was a small sampling, the results were consistent with experience all over the country. The citizen with a gun has a much better chance of defending him or herself. The statistics collected by the U.S. Department of Justice on criminal victimization show that firearms are more effective than other means of self-protection, such as trying to reason with the offender.[1]

You can confirm this by collecting your own news reports for a few months. Count the number of armed citizens killed and compare this with the number of unarmed victims. You'll find that:

A. Your chances are much better if you're armed. The sight of the gun may stop the attack, without firing a shot. If there's shooting, you'll probably survive.

B. If you're unarmed you're at the attacker's mercy. You may think that you'll be okay if you just give him your wallet, but what if he's a rapist? What if he wants to rape your wife or daughter? What if he kills you to eliminate a witness? There are "thrill killers" who rob and then kill just for "kicks."

C. There's a slight risk of killing the wrong person or of having a tragic accident with a gun. This happens, and let's not pretend it doesn't. There are precautions to take to prevent this. Practicing gun safety and learning good tactics help prevent accidents.

Actually, having a gun for protection is pretty safe. About 50 thousand people die in traffic accidents each year. Only about two thousand people die from gun accidents.

If you're afraid of guns, or religious scruples prevent you from using one in self-defense, you shouldn't have a gun. They're not for everyone. Instead, arm yourself with a club or other weapon, and hope for the best.

NOTES

1. *Criminal Victimization in the United States,* 1983, U. S. Department of Justice, Bureau of Justice Statistics, p. 70.

THE THREATS

In planning for defense it helps to know something about the threats you may face. Not all threats occur in all situations. Some are more likely to face you at work, and others will seek you out at home. Let's take a quick look at some types.

BURGLARS

They can strike anywhere and everywhere. There are roughly two types, professional and amateur. The "pro" is a career criminal with experience and proficiency who "hits" targets worthy of his skill. These are businesses, homes in wealthy neighborhoods, and high-priced hotels. The "pro" is capable and determined, and most passive defense measures won't stop him. Because he's skilled, he can work his way past almost any type of alarm you might have.

The amateur is usually a teenager starting out on his criminal career. He also may be doing it on impulse or just for fun. He's not very selective, and may hit anywhere. Alarms and "Operation Identification" stickers will often deter him. He looks for the easy jobs. He's the type who'll walk around a neighborhood looking for a door that's been left open.

It's a cliche that burglars go about their business unarmed. Don't bet your life on it. It might be your last mistake.

Burglars prefer to "hit" when the premises are unoccupied. They want to avoid interference, but if you arrive while the burglary's in progress and surprise them, you may be in great danger. Likewise if the burglar breaks in unaware that you're on the premises.

ROBBERS

Robbers are bold and strike everywhere: home, business, on the street, etc. There are several types of robbers. Strong-arm robbers are what we call "muggers," and depend on physical strength to do the job. These are the ones who prey on the weak and elderly. Purse-snatchers are muggers. So are the ones who steal Social Security checks from old ladies.

The armed robber uses a knife, gun, or club. He may rob individuals or businesses. The robber who ambushes individuals is usually the lower-class type who "harvests" targets of opportunity and settles for what he can get. The more ambitious and able robber goes after businesses because that's usually where the money is. Because of the nature of his crime, he's always in a hurry.

Robbers can be very bold. Some commit robberies even in the midst of crowds. One pair accosted victims in New York department stores. One would step in front of the victim, blocking the way. The other would poke the victim from behind with a gun or knife and murmur "Give him your money." The victim was often too surprised to resist, and the robbers got away by vanishing into the crowds.

Robbers rarely strike residences, but in Eastern cities there are some forced entries, followed by robberies. Strict gun control laws ensure that most citizens are disarmed. However, robbers find guns easily on the black market.

PERVERTS

This class includes all sexually-motivated attackers. Peeping Toms are nonviolent, but a prowler may be more sinister than a Peeping Tom. He may be a rapist or thrill-killer looking for a way in.

Rapists can be very violent. The run-of-the-mill "date rape" artist is unpleasant to his victim, but he doesn't compare to the bashing and mutilating rapist who seeks out strangers.

Child molesters are usually non-violent, and even gentle. The vicious child-murderer is rare.

Exhibitionists, also known as "flashers" and "wienie waggers," are nuisances. They're nonviolent.

Sex criminals strike in many places, but not usually in crowds. The "flashers" and subway "rubbers," are annoying, but nonviolent, and you can't open fire on them. The subway rubber works in a crowd, and depends upon his victim's being too embarrassed to protest. The domain of the violent sex criminal is typically the lonely place; a vacant subway car, a dark street, or a residence with a lone occupant.

KIDNAPERS

Kidnapers are special cases. They won't bother you unless you're wealthy.

DRUNKS AND ROWDIES

Obviously, you usually find these in bars. This is a problem if you own or work in a bar. Some bars have reputations for gunfights and stabbings.

Drunks sometimes make stupid and threatening statements. It's important to remain calm when confronting this sort of person and not let yourself be stampeded into over-reacting. One bar owner took a drunken client at face value when he threatened to go out to his car, get a gun, and kill him. He fired first and spent a couple of years in prison. The drunk turned out to have been unarmed.

THRILL KILLERS

The odds of running into one of these are small. Unfortunately, if you do, you'll be in deep trouble. You won't be able to meekly hand over your wallet and say that you don't want trouble. Thrill killers don't take prisoners. For you, it will be simply "kill or be killed."

What makes thrill killers so dangerous is that they initially masquerade as less dangerous types. They act like burglars, muggers, or armed robbers of the ordinary sort. You may think that it's just another hold-up until they tie you up or put handcuffs on you. When it gets past this point, it's too late.

This should be a powerful incentive for you to avoid taking any chances with a criminal. If the situation justifies it, use deadly force.

STATISTICS

Adding up figures from various sources and projecting them as a whole, Americans have a 1 in 400 chance of getting murdered during an average lifespan. This risk isn't evenly distributed. Some groups and some areas are far riskier than others. FBI statistics show a murder rate in 1985 of 8 persons per 100,000 in Arizona. The rate in California is 1.5 per 100,000, and Michigan has a rate of 11.2. Although New York State has an overall rate of 9.5 per 100,000, certain areas of New York City are like the Twilight Zone. In Harlem, 1 resident in 500 dies violently each year. Among young black males living in Harlem, the murder rate is 1 in 100.

Other crimes are much more frequent. Assault, robbery, and other violent crimes are common almost everywhere. Property crimes are common even in locales with little violent crime. There are many millions of burglaries, robberies, and other property crimes each year, and sooner or later one will happen to you.

PASSIVE AND ACTIVE DEFENSE

When you're attacked by a criminal, crime becomes your business. Taking steps to protect yourself and your property means accepting your responsibility towards yourself and towards society.

There are two types of defensive actions, active and passive. Active means directly countering the criminal to stop him from completing his crime. Passive techniques deter or obstruct him without any direct action from you. You don't even have to be there.

Passive means include locks, bars on windows, alarm systems, and avoidance tactics such as not using the subway. Passive tactics also include not carrying much cash, and keeping valuables in a safe deposit box. Locking your car and notifying the police when you go on vacation are also passive tactics, aimed at reducing your risks and losses.

Active techniques include physically fighting an attacker, with or without a weapon, and preparations directed towards that end, such as setting up protected firing positions and laying out fields of fire.

Both active and passive methods have their place. Both can help protect you. Taking defensive steps is much more reasonable than relying on the police to protect you. The police are a reactive force, taking reports after the fact and trying to track down the perpetrator. Street patrol doesn't help much. A street cop can go for many years before he comes across a crime in progress.

Some departments take "pro-active" measures, such as stake-outs and "sting" operations. These are more successful, but still only a drop in the bucket.

You, the citizen, are the first line of defense against crime. In many cases, simple passive defense will protect lives and property. Sometimes, it requires armed force. For example, in the several Manson murders, none of the victims were armed. They were slaughtered. What might have happened if even one victim had been armed? Perhaps as little as one shot might have prevented several killings.

In defense against crime, it's usually: "If you want something done right, do it yourself."

There's another aspect that we rarely hear discussed. Passive measures such as locks and grills don't by themselves deter crime. A burglar who sees them on your property will seek a target with less protection. All you've really done is to send the problem over to your neighbor's premises.

Active, armed defense is positive. If you shoot an armed robber, you end his career on the spot. Deadly force is the final solution.

WEAPONS

The gun is the core of the subject. If you don't own one, you'll need to study this chapter carefully to obtain the groundwork for choosing one. If your hobby is guns, this will be the most interesting part of the book.

WHICH TYPE OF WEAPON IS BEST?

Each gun hobbyist or professional gunhandler has his favorite weapon, and some have very strong opinions based more on emotion than on logic. Some feel that handguns are the only way to go. Others prefer the greater throw-weight of shotguns. Every type of firearm has its advocates, and you can be sure that the friends you ask will give you different answers.

For self-defense, almost any firearm will do, depending on the situation. The overriding fact is that we're not all gun collectors, and we can't afford, at today's prices, to buy whatever weapon a gun expert writing a magazine article tells us is the best weapon. Making the choice is even more difficult because of the contradictory advice available.

You have to make the final choice, based on the information in this chapter and what you read in other sources. Be sure you make your decision on practicality, without regard to any artificial glamour attached to certain weapons. One practical factor to consider is concealment. Do you need to carry a weapon with you, or are you concerned only about home defense? A shoulder weapon will do very well for home defense, but is impractical for concealed carry.

The first, and major fact about making a choice is that many people who use a weapon for defense have only one. This is true even of police officers. Many private citizens also can't afford to maintain an arsenal.

The gun you have is the one with which you go to war. That's the way it is. Don't worry too much over whether you made the right choice because you've read about the fabulous firepower available with a new Super-Magnum featured in the current issue of a gun magazine.

The weapon should suit the situation and the tactics. If you already have a weapon, adapt your tactics to suit it. If you already have several weapons, you'll find that one is a better choice than the others for your purposes.

Let's look at the characteristics of weapons before making a choice, considering the most important features first:

Reliability. This is, by far, the first and most important characteristic. The weapon must fire when you need it to; no jams, hang-ups, or hitches allowed. The most powerful weapon in the world won't help you if it jams when you need it. A cranky and temperamental gun can cost a target shooter points in a match. If you're shooting for real, it can cost you your life.

Some people disagree over which type of gun is the most reliable. Revolver lovers say auto pistols jam. Auto pistol fans point out that revolvers don't pass the army acceptance tests, which check reliability after immersion in a mud bath. The truth is that any weapon can malfunction, given poor ammunition and poor care.

What all of this means to you is that, if you're choosing a weapon for protection, don't take anyone's word that it works well. Check it out yourself. Fire at least two boxes of the ammo you intend to use. This will give you a good idea of how the weapon works with that particular ammo.

Ammunition is very important. Some guns digest one brand or type of ammo very well, but get constipated with another. This is true of both auto pistols and revolvers.

Keeping the weapon clean helps reliability. Clean the weapon thoroughly before firing, and keep it clean thereafter. The instructions packed with the gun show you how. Never assume that it's clean when you take it out of the box. Also, never assume that it will fire because it's new. There are new product defects with weapons, just as with cars.

Buy enough ammo to cover your practice needs and leave some over for real. Don't, above all, practice with one type of ammunition and load the weapon with another type for defense without first testing it to make sure it works well in your weapon. If you decide to use a less expensive brand of practice ammo, test-fire some of the defense loads you'll be using to make sure that they work in that weapon.

If your choice is a shoulder weapon, the variety available is even greater than with handguns. Just remember that all types of actions can fail, and all can be made to work reliably.

Whatever your choice, there's a trouble-shooting procedure if you run into persistent jams. Follow these steps in the order listed:

1. Clean the weapon. If this doesn't work, then
2. Change your ammunition. If this still doesn't help, then
3. Take the weapon to a gunsmith or get another gun.

If you're skilled in gun repair, you may be able to solve the problem yourself. If you're not, employ a gunsmith for help.

Accuracy. The weapon must be accurate enough to hit your target at normal gunfighting ranges. Most weapons from reputable manufacturers are more accurate than most shooters, but we occasionally find a lemon. There are weapons that shoot several feet off at short ranges, and this can be enough to miss a man-size target. Always check for accuracy when test-firing a weapon.

It's important to understand that "accuracy" means practical accuracy in your hands. There are sophisticated ways of test-firing weapons from devices, such as a Ransom Machine Rest, that clamp the weapon in place to eliminate human error. These are valuable, as intrinsic accuracy is a good indicator of quality, but the results are not the last word as far as accuracy for defense is concerned.

Let's define accuracy for your needs: Acceptable accuracy is the ability to hit a man-size silhouette at the longest range at which you're going to have to open fire. For home defense, measure the longest distance in your house, such as the diagonal of the largest room, or the distance down the longest corridor.

The weapon's grip might not be right for you. The weapon might be too heavy, or the sights may be wrong for your eyes. You need to check all of these out before making a final decision.

Remember that you are part of the picture. If you're a novice shot, don't blame the gun. You might have to develop your skill some more.

Closely related to accuracy is "pointability." This means that the weapon points at your target naturally, without strain. Not all weapons "point" equally well for different people. Some handguns are too big for most hands, or they point so poorly that accuracy is possible only by experts using a two-handed grip.

One quick test to check a weapon's "pointing" in your hands is the closed-eyes test. Make sure the weapon's empty, then pick a spot on the wall across the room. Bring the weapon up until you're sighting on that target. If necessary, adjust your stance until you're comfortable. Now repeat the exercise. Holding the weapon down at your side, close your eyes. Bring the weapon up until you feel it's pointed at the target. Open your eyes. Is it lined up closely enough to hit? Do this with several weapons to find the one that "points" best for you.

While it's not the purpose of this book to advertise brands of weapons, there are some models that have proven to be unusually reliable and which are accepted by many people. This doesn't mean that you should restrict your choice to one of these, but at least give them a close look when making a choice:

A. SIG pistols, Models 220, (45 ACP), and the 9mm models 225, 226, and the .380 ACP Model 230. These are expensive, but very well-made and reliable. One significant feature is that these pistols have no external safeties. It's all done inside, and they're safe to carry without having to put on a safety. They're ready to fire with a pull of the trigger.

B. Smith & Wesson Model 10 .38 Special revolver, a good basic model that's been around since the turn of the century.

C. Ruger Speed Six, a six-shot .357 Magnum revolver for people with small hands.

D. Glock Model 17, a 9mm auto pistol that's moderately priced, points well, and is unusually reliable. Like the SIG, this has only internal safeties. It can't go off accidentally, and firing takes only a pull on the trigger.

E. Ruger GP-100, a top quality .357 Magnum revolver that's both elegant and reliable. This also comes in stainless steel.

In shoulder weapons, there are some good choices:

F. Mossberg 500 shotgun, 12-gauge. This is a moderately priced, but very reliable weapon. This one has a Choate Folding Stock.

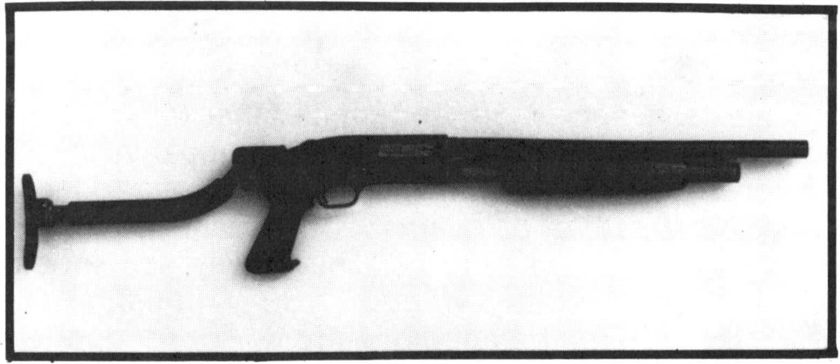

G. Remington Model 870 shotgun, 12-gauge. This is the choice of many police agencies.

H. Ruger Model 10/22 carbine. This is a low-cost, reliable carbine in caliber .22 Long Rifle, useful for both plinking and for defense. This weapon works best with CCI Stinger ammunition.

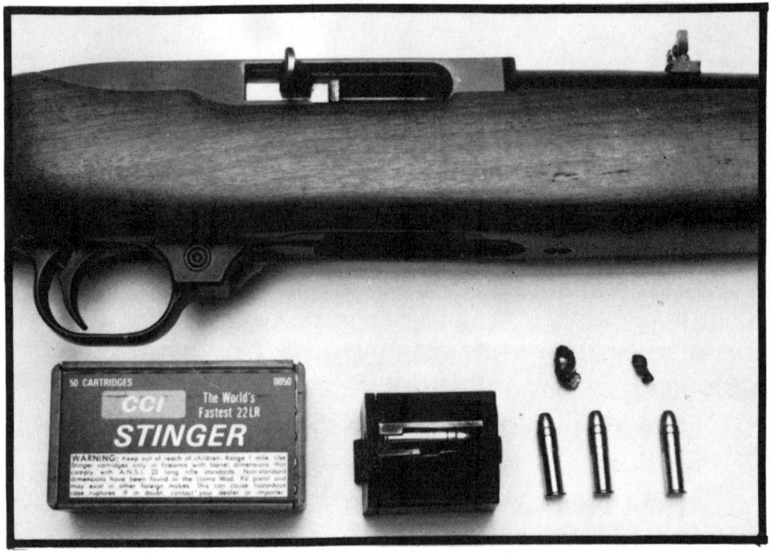

I. Remington Nylon 66 carbine, again in .22 Long Rifle.

This list is very short, and omits other good choices. Remember, though, that every company has its lemons. The American manufacturers have had more than their share of problems recently, and workmanship isn't what it used to be. This is why you should examine closely any weapon you're considering. Take it out of the box and dry-fire it. Ask for another of the same model, and try that one. Pick the one that's smoother.

Instead of buying a defense weapon in a discount store, consider buying it from an established gun dealer. They know more about the products than department store clerks, and they're in a better position to stand behind what they sell. Ask the gunsmith what to do if the weapon malfunctions when you take it out for test-firing. If he tells you to return it to the manufacturer, don't buy it there. That's discount store policy. A good gunsmith or gun dealer should be able to take care of such problems on the spot, or at least give you another gun.

Caliber. This is the subject that generates the most controversy. Which caliber is best? The answer you get depends on who you ask. To some, their favorite caliber is like religion. Any challenge to it is sacrilegious, like an insult to their mothers or wives. This is particularly true of devotees of the .45 ACP, who look upon anyone who challenges their choice with the same attitude they'd have towards a child molester.

The hard fact is that people have been injured and killed with every caliber made. If you look at the facts, and only the facts, you can make a good case for every caliber.

You can say that a certain caliber is very powerful. You can also point out that the .22 Long Rifle cartridge is very inexpensive, allowing you to buy more ammo for practice. The 9mm Luger is available all over the world, while the .45 ACP is popular mainly in the United States. All depends on your point of view.

Closely related to caliber is "stopping power." This topic is so misunderstood that the arguments about stopping power go on and on without really settling anything. Stopping power means the power to stop an opponent. The question is; "How quickly?" As we'll see, the instant stop is largely a myth.

A .357 Magnum makes a jug full of water burst with the shock of impact. Keep this effect in mind, because the human body is about 95% water.

Putting down an adversary with gunfire is mainly hitting him in the right spot. A shot in the brain or spinal cord will do it, whatever the caliber. It's hard to aim so precisely in a gunfight so the usual practice is to aim for the trunk, the largest area of the body and therefore the easiest to hit.

There are many vital organs, such as the heart and lungs, in the trunk, and many major blood vessels. This helps the chances of inflicting a serious and incapacitating injury.

One viewpoint is that you should use the largest caliber available to inflict the maximal injury wherever you hit. This is substituting bullet power for skill, and it brings one serious problem. Whatever caliber you choose, you have to be able to place your shots accurately to do the job. If the caliber is too powerful for you to handle, because of weapon weight and recoil, it won't do you any good. Not everyone can handle the larger calibers. More importantly, many can't handle the larger calibers well enough to shoot accurately and quickly in a life-threatening situation. This is why the smaller calibers will always have their place.

The other fact about stopping power is that unless you hit your opponent in a spot that causes instant unconsciousness or paralysis, such as the brain or spine, it'll take several seconds for the effect of the wound to put him down. This is true even of fatal injuries, and has given us the phrase, "The dead man's five seconds." This is an important point to remember, because a dying suspect can still kill you if you give him the opportunity.

In assessing the seriousness of a wound, we have to calculate the human element. An attacker who takes a body hit may go down immediately or continue firing at you for seconds, minutes, or even hours. It depends on the exact site of the hit, how big he is, his physical and emotional stamina, and other factors, such as whether he's on drugs. Suspects on drugs can sometimes withstand horrible injuries, and don't collapse until they die.

We can sketch a few rules of thumb. A burglar taking a solid torso hit without expecting it will probably go down quickly. On the other hand, if someone's actually attacking you in a frenzy, with the adrenalin pumping hard, he won't go down as easily. You might have to empty your weapon into him and he still might not go down. There have been documented cases of people taking several large caliber hits with handguns, and even shotguns and rifles, and not going down immediately.

You also have to consider range and penetration. Up close, you don't need a long-range weapon. Long range can work against you if the bullet travels on to endanger innocent people. Likewise, over-penetration is hazardous in a built-up area because a stray bullet can go through several walls. You can cut down over-penetration by the right choice of ammunition, but some weapons are still unsuited for some uses.

Concealability. You won't have to worry about this if your main concern is home defense or carrying the weapon in a car or truck. If you must carry your weapon on your person, you'll need a concealable weapon, which means a handgun. In some situations, you may carry a rifle or shotgun on a sling under an overcoat.

It's easy to conceal a pistol, depending on your clothing. If you wear only a shirt and pants, as in summer, you have to hide the weapon's outline under the shirt or inside your pants. A small pistol might be all you can manage. If you wear tight pants, you'll have a real problem.

A sweater or jacket help a lot. They allow concealing a much larger weapon.

Do you need a holster or not? There's no clear answer for civilians. Police officers are required to carry their handguns in holsters, but you're free to do what's best for you. If you're wearing a heavy jacket, it might be best to carry the weapon in an outside pocket. Drawing it from a holster under your coat will take longer than from the pocket.

If you read many gun magazines, you might think that holsters are essential, and you might feel naked without one. Don't worry about it. Guns existed long before holsters were invented, and in Europe and many other places, people carry pistols in pockets more than they do in holsters.

Firepower. This relates to the number of shots you can fire in a given time. Many people feel that the faster they can shoot, the better, but this isn't really as important as making the shots count. Doing it right with the first shot or two is much better than pouring in the lead over a long time. In fact, an important reason to avoid protracted shoot-outs is the danger from stray shots and ricochets.

Semi-auto weapons are the fastest shooting. Yes, it's true that full-auto weapons are even faster, but so few people have them that we won't consider them here. A skilled shot can send the bullets out of a revolver barrel very quickly, too, but the music ends after six shots.

In rifles and shotguns, auto-loaders are the quickest to fire, with slide-actions and lever-actions in second place. Bolt-actions are somewhat slower. The difference between them is not very great, and in fact is less than the difference between someone who is skilled at working the actions, and another who hasn't practiced at all.

Ease of Reloading. Like firepower, this isn't as important as it seems. It's convenient to have a weapon that reloads quickly, but gunfights rarely take more than a few shots. If you exhaust one of the new 17-round auto pistols and haven't yet put your opponent down, you're in more trouble than a spare magazine will help.

Auto pistols are always the fastest in reloading. There are speed-loaders for revolvers, but they still can only load six at a time. Single-action revolvers, loading through a gate in the frame, are painfully slow in reloading.

RIFLES

Rifles are the most common type of weapon made. They're usually between 32" and 45" long and weigh from 5 to 10 lbs. There are heavier and lighter ones, and some short carbines and extra-long elephant guns, but they're not common. Rifles fire cartridges from the small .22 rimfires to the extra-large and powerful Magnums.

Their size and weight make them hard to conceal. Rifles usually have more power than you need or want, sending bullets accurately for many hundreds of yards. The excessive range and penetration make for great danger to innocent people living nearby.

If you decide on a rifle for home defense, be careful to select fields of fire that don't endanger innocent people. You can also help reduce the danger by selecting a lighter load. If you hand-load, you can tailor the load to your exact need.

Rifles are best used for shooting at far away targets and at motor vehicles. Unless you're facing an unusual situation, you're not likely to need to do either.

A rifle can be convenient if you don't have to carry it on the person. In a vehicle, it can be a formidable and easily available weapon if carried on the rear seat or in a rack. The rifle's size is a handicap if you need defense against a close assailant because it's easier and quicker to bring a pistol up in a car than a shoulder weapon.

The rifle has two huge advantages. It's easier to learn to shoot than a pistol, and the bullets do much more damage than do handgun bullets. Still, other weapons add up to more advantages for many situations, as we'll see when we examine them.

SHOTGUNS

Many prefer shotguns because of their many advantages, despite their weight and bulk. If concealment isn't important, a shotgun is ideal. The shotgun also packs a hard punch at close range but doesn't send its projectiles very far. At point-blank range, any sort of load in a shotgun hits harder than a magnum handgun, but the range is far less than a pistol bullet's.

For defensive purposes, we'll consider only the 12-gauge. Other gauges will do the job, but not quite as well, and the 12-gauge is a police standard. This gauge shotgun delivers between one and two thousand foot-pounds of muzzle energy, enough for almost any purpose.

Depending on the load, the effective range can vary between 30 feet and over 100 yards. A rifle slug carries to well over 100 yards, depending on the slug, the weapon, and the shooter. A charge of number eight birdshot is deadly at very short range but at 30 feet or so it loses enough power so that it won't go through both sides of an interior wall. This is very important to remember when thinking about defense in built-up areas.

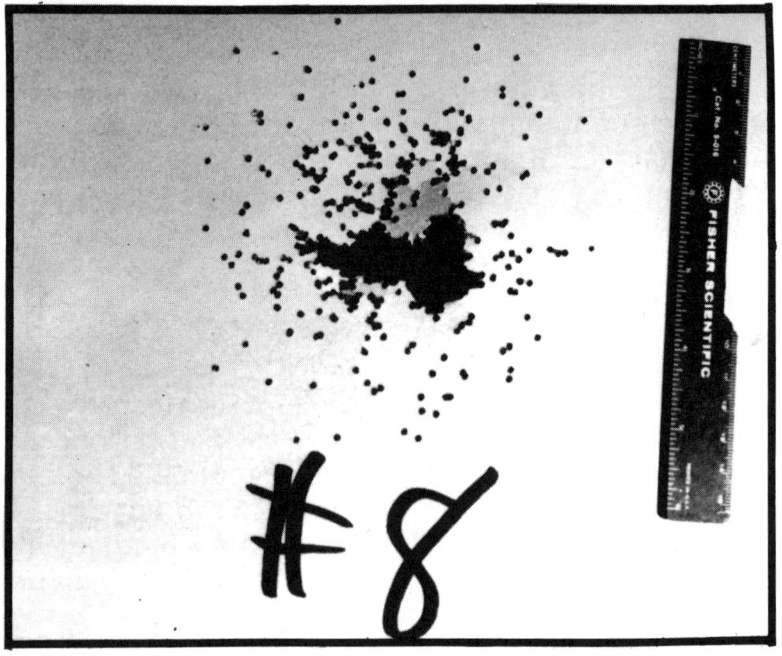

A load of number eight birdshot at ten feet. This nasty penetration of an interior wall is called a "rat-hole," and gives an idea of what it would do on a suspect. At 30 feet the shot have spread and lost enough velocity so that they don't penetrate all the way through the wall.

It's important to understand how shotguns pattern. Contrary to what some people think, projectiles from a shotgun don't spread out fan-wise as soon as they leave the muzzle. They stay together for a distance, depending on the type of load and whether or not the barrel has a choke on it. Dispersion is very gradual, with most pellets hitting a man-size figure at thirty yards. This means you still have to aim or point the shotgun accurately, not just point it in the target's general direction. The spread allows very little margin for error at normal gunfighting distances.

Rear view of the wall, showing the exit hole of a column of number eight birdshot.

A shotgun is a true short-range weapon. At ranges greater than ten yards, you run into problems. A light load with good dispersion at short range spreads too much and loses velocity too quickly to be effective at longer ranges. A shell with nine pellets of double-ought buckshot, heavier pellets which retain their velocity out to fifty yards, has too few to deliver a dense pattern on the target at that range.

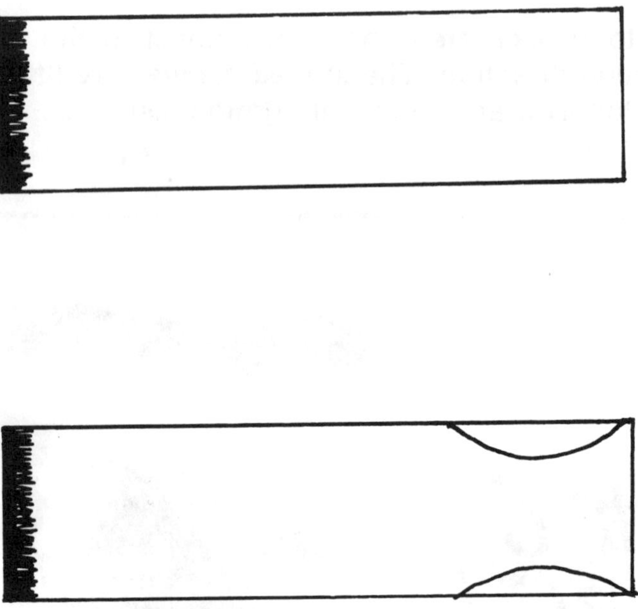

The cylindrical bore, top, allows the shot column to pass without tightening it. You get the quickest dispersion from a cylindrical bore. A choke, bottom, tightens the shot column, and the pattern holds together out to a greater range than otherwise.

Ammo manufacturers make "rifled slugs" for shotguns. These are heavy cylinders of soft lead that resemble large bullets. When you fire such a load from a shotgun, you're really working with a smoothbore musket. Technical improvements in slugs allow an expert with a shotgun equipped with rifle sights can hit a target at 100 yards or more, but slugs penetrate too much for most household use.

The best combination for home defense is a pump-action shotgun such as the Mossberg 500, and shells loaded with number eight birdshot. This is as close to perfect as you're going to find in a shotgun, devastating to an intruder, yet safe to use indoors. The one drawback is that if you need to shoot an intruder through a wall, you'll have to put the muzzle right up against the wall to ensure penetration.

Twelve gauge is standard, but if it's too powerful in recoil for you, a sixteen is still fairly hefty. Twenty-gauge is smaller yet, and a .410 still delivers more power than a .41 Magnum revolver.

HANDGUNS

These are the most glamorous weapons, partly because they're the ones most often seen on TV and the movie screen. Their macho image appeals to many people, although they're the feeblest of firearms. They're also the most difficult to learn to shoot. Moreover, handguns are the objects of most of the gun control laws in this country, making them harder to obtain in some locales.

With all that, handguns have advantages that make them preferable for some defensive uses. While you're usually better off with a shoulder weapon for offensive use, circumstances often force you to choose a pistol for defense. Concealability is important when traveling, for example, when a shotgun or carbine under your arm would attract unwanted attention. If you're a storekeeper, carrying a shotgun slung over your shoulder would cause raised eyebrows among your customers. If you keep a shoulder weapon in a closet or behind a counter, an armed robber wouldn't give you a chance to get to it, but a handgun under the jacket or sweater is much more available. In a car, a handgun can lie on the seat next to you, immediately at hand.

Much misinformation has appeared about pistols because of their aura. It's hard to believe that writers could perpetuate such myths, but it happens. One is that a .357 Magnum bullet will shatter a car's engine block. It might penetrate or cause a crack if it hits where the metal is thinnest, but it won't shatter an engine block, not even a motorcycle engine. Another myth is that auto pistols jam, while revolvers don't. This isn't true, either, and it's been demonstrably false for almost eighty years. The U.S. Army tests during the first decade of this century showed that the Colt auto pistol was more reliable than the revolvers of the era. Today, almost all armies in the world use auto pistols.

The most important fact regarding weapon reliability is the use and care it gets. If you take care of your weapon, clean it regularly, use the right ammunition, and avoid doing something stupid, it will give you good service. On the other hand, you can jam the best weapon in the world by careless use and by ignoring maintenance.

A revolver is a handgun which holds cartridges in a rotating cylinder that lines up each cartridge with the barrel for firing. It usually holds six cartridges, but some .22 caliber revolvers hold as many as nine. The mechanism is fragile, compared to auto pistols, but the revolver works well most of the time unless dirt gets in through one of the many openings.

An auto pistol is also called a self-loader, or automatic. It holds cartridges in a magazine, sometimes called a clip, although this term is technically incorrect. The magazine fits into the handle, or grip. The top part of the pistol is called the slide, and comes back after each shot. A small hook, the extractor, pulls the fired shell from the chamber and a small stud, called an ejector, throws it out. Returning forward, the slide picks up a fresh cartridge from the magazine and rams it into the chamber. This mechanism is simpler than the revolver's, but is more sensitive to the quality of ammunition.

A revolver will digest almost any ammunition you feed it because the mechanism works by your finger on the trigger. If a cartridge doesn't fire, pressing the trigger again rotates the cylinder and brings a fresh one into line. An auto pistol uses the power of the cartridge to work the action. A weak cartridge won't push the slide back far enough to work the action.

Opinions vary regarding whether the revolver is easier to learn to use than the automatic. The experts disagree on this point, and your best course is to try each type and make up your own mind.

In both types of handgun, there are two types of actions. One is called the single-action because the trigger only releases the hammer or striker, and it's necessary to cock it before firing. The double-action, or self-cocker, works the hammer or striker with one pull of the trigger.

Opinions also vary regarding the value of the single- versus the double-action mechanisms. In revolvers, police officers have accepted the double-action since the first, about a century ago. In auto pistols, the single-action design has been the favorite of many people, but the trend has been steadily towards the double-action. The specification for the new U.S. military pistols has been a double-action automatic, and the armed forces adopted the Beretta Model 92SB-F.

Regarding cartridge power, there's a wide choice in both revolvers and autos. Both types are made for the smallest calibers to the largest magnums, and the biggest ones are more powerful than you're likely to need.

For just plain firepower, the auto pistol is clearly superior. Most automatics hold more than the six rounds which are standard in large-caliber revolvers. Some hold as many as 17 or 18 in the magazine. With one in the chamber, that's a lot of metal to throw without reloading.

Do you really need the extra firepower? Some say "yes," and others disagree. Let's try to settle this question right now.

Most gunfights are over after just a few shots. If you happen to be caught in one that requires more, you'll be happy to have the extra firepower. The extra rounds are like insurance. You hope that you'll never have to use it, but it's comforting to know it's there. The military prefer large-capacity auto pistols because battles last for much longer than civilian shootouts.

The way you reload each type of weapon is significant. Revolvers have cylinders, and the double-action types swing out to let you eject the fired cases and insert fresh ones. A great drawback of single-action revolvers, although some people use them for defense, is the extreme slowness of reloading. You have to open a loading gate in the frame, and rotate the cylinder manually to let you eject each shell as it comes into position. You then have to insert fresh cartridges one by one. Double-action revolvers allow you to insert two or three at a time, whatever you can hold between your fingers. There are speedloaders which hold six rounds, allowing you to insert a full load in one pass.

A Smith & Wesson Model 10, with a speedloader made by HKS. This allows quick one-step reloading of a revolver with six fresh cartridges.

All auto pistols have magazines, and this speeds up reloading a lot. Because the automatic ejects the fired cases, you don't have to, and you need only press a button on the side to eject the clip. You insert a fresh one, work the slide once to chamber a fresh round, and you're in business again.

Another point about reloading systems is that it's hard to reload revolvers partially if you've only fired a couple of rounds and want to top up before going on. You have to open the cylinder, extract the fired shells one by one, and then replace them one by one. Another way to do it is to dump all shells, fired or not, into your hand, pick out the unfired cartridges and put them in your pocket, and discard the rest. You reload the revolver with a speedloader. Partly reloading an automatic involves only removing the magazine, and replacing it with a full one. You can always replace the first magazine later, if you need a few more shots. This takes far less time, and provides a greater ready supply of ammunition than reloading a revolver.

WHICH WEAPON FOR YOU?

You'll need to do a lot of thinking about this if you don't already have a weapon you like. Before you lay out your hard-earned dollars, look into this very carefully. If some of your friends have weapons, ask if you can fire them, to see for yourself how well they work in your hands.

AMMUNITION

Whichever weapon you have, it's only as good as what you feed it. There's enough of a variety of ammunition available to make some good choices.

The first question to consider is whether you should reload for defense or use factory ammo. If you're not a reloader, you don't have to consider this. If you are, you can hand-tailor your loads for your purposes, but you have to keep one important aspect in mind: Do you reload well enough to trust your life to your own loads?

While reloading need not be a very complicated task, if you're going to use your hand-loads for defense they should be good enough to work every time. Unfortunately, a lot can go wrong with handloading, even though the process is simple in principle. If you can't produce reloads that fire 100 times out of 100 cartridges, don't trust your life to them. Use factory ammo for defense, and save your handloads for low-cost practice.

SHOTGUN

We've already seen that the number eight birdshot load is very convenient for active defense indoors without the danger of penetration through interior walls. If you live in a rural area, you might try another load if you're not concerned about where your shot eventually lands. Number four buckshot consists of 27 pellets ¼" in diameter, which will provide a dense enough pattern out to several dozen yards. Double-ought buckshot, which many police departments like, is effective only at close range because there are too few pellets to give a dense pattern at longer ranges.

This is not counting magnum loads. There are loads available which pack more punch, but these may be too heavy for you. Federal Cartridge Company provides a truly effective 15-pellet double-ought load, but this requires a shotgun chambered for 3" magnum shotshells, and the recoil is very heavy.

Loading the weapon with slugs allows use of the shotgun as a smoothbore musket. The heavy lead slugs have a lot of punch, and don't disperse the way a shot pattern does. A slug requires careful aiming, and overall a shotgun loaded with slugs isn't as accurate as a rifle. However, a shotgun offers much more versatility than a rifle, because it accepts a great variety of ammunition.

RIFLES

Almost any hunting bullet will do for a center-fire rifle such as a .243 or a .308. All will deliver accurate fire out to several hundred yards. This sort of performance is useful mainly in rural areas, where targets may be far away and there are no innocent people who might be hit accidentally.

A special load good for short ranges is the Remington Accelerator load. This fires a .22 caliber jacketed hollow-point bullet from a 30-caliber weapon by means of a plastic casing called a "sabot," which guides it down the bore and then falls off when out of the muzzle. The small bullet travels at velocities exceeding 3000 fps, depending on the cartridge and length of the barrel. A .30-30 won't propel the bullet as fast, but a .308 or .30-06 will send it at well over 3000 fps. This gives the bullet explosive impact when it hits. If it hits a wall, it will expand and slow down greatly, instead of traveling on for hundreds of yards.

Rimfire rifles, using .22 caliber cartridges, are another story. One excellent round for .22 rimfires is the CCI Stinger, a jacketed hollow-point which typically comes out of the muzzle at about 1500 fps. The expansion that this bullet delivers is awesome. At close range, bullets fragment upon impact, which causes severe wounds.

HANDGUNS

Pistol ammunition is the most controversial. Part of the reason is that the handgun is a marginal weapon. It doesn't have the range of the rifle, nor does it have the power of the shoulder weapon, rifle or shotgun.

This is why, when firing on an attacker with a handgun, always fire at least two shots. Make it standard practice to fire in bursts of two. Two shots actually have more effect than just double of one shot. Unless you hit the same organ twice, you're disrupting two life support systems, and your attacker has double trouble and the effect of shock to make it worse. The effects of hitting two life support systems snowball, and the combined effect will put him down much more quickly than if you'd fired only one shot.

The most common answer to the problem of power is to enhance the performance of the ammunition with a high-speed hollow-point bullet. The hollow-point makes the bullet expand upon impact, which delivers maximum disruptive energy to the target. The mushroom effect ensures that the bullets tear a jagged and gaping hole, instead of slipping smoothly through.

The mushroom effect helps if the bullets hit a wall. They expand and lose their aerodynamic shape, which helps reduce over-travel. If they strike a solid wall, which they don't penetrate, they tend to fragment, and the small pieces don't fly as far as an intact bullet would.

There are hollow-points made in all common handgun calibers. They don't work equally well. The reason is that a hollow-point bullet needs to travel at about 1000 fps or more to expand reliably. 1000 fps seems to be the threshold of expansion, and bullets traveling much slower than this rarely expand.

The modern formula is a jacketed high-speed hollow-point bullet. The high speed is necessary for reliable expansion. The hollow-point helps the mushroom effect, and the hard metal bullet jacket ensures that the bullet grips the rifling as it travels down the barrel.

There are exceptions. One of them is in caliber .38 Special.

This is the Speer .38 caliber hollow-base wadcutter bullet, made of pure lead. When handloaded backward, with 5 grains of Unique powder, the expansion is double the nominal diameter. The soft lead mushrooms to almost ¾". The bullet, when loaded hollow cavity forward, is very unstable, and sometimes strikes sideways. This causes it to flatten out, and still produces a jagged wound.

Other .38 Special loads, including all factory loads, use jacketed hollow-points, also known as "JHP." These vary in weight from 95 grains to 180 grains. Most people who use a .38 Special, like the bullets that range between 95 grains and 125 grains.

Because the .38 Special is an old cartridge, it carries a relatively modest powder charge, suitable for the old weapons for which it was designed many decades ago. Because there have been significant advances in metallurgy and gun-building techniques, modern revolvers can take pressure levels that the old ones can't.

This is why ammunition manufacturers produce modern versions of the old .38 Special, loaded to higher pressures. These are popularly called "+P" loads, the symbol meaning "additional pressure." These cartridges are made only for modern firearms in good condition, and are used by police. They have the "+P" on the headstamp.

There's an additional pressure level made in .38 Special, but these cartridges are intended for restricted distribution to law enforcement agencies only. They're headstamped "+P+" and fire JHP bullets at velocities and pressures between the .38 Special and the .357 Magnum. They're actually not designed for use in .38 Specials, but .357 Magnum revolvers. Many law officers prefer the slightly heavier and stronger .357 Magnum revolvers, but don't like the recoil and muzzle blast of the full-power cartridge. The "+P+" cartridges fill this need.

If you happen to obtain some of these cartridges, look for the headstamp to confirm that they're actually "+P+." If you have a good-quality .38 Special revolver in top condition, you can fire these cartridges safely. Otherwise, use them in a Smith Model 19 or a Ruger Security-Six, both of which are made for .357 Magnum.

In caliber 9mm Luger, there's relatively little problem in making bullets expand. Bullets normally leave the muzzle at over 1000 fps. Some of the lighter bullets, the 90-grain JHPs, travel at about 1300 fps, well over the threshold.

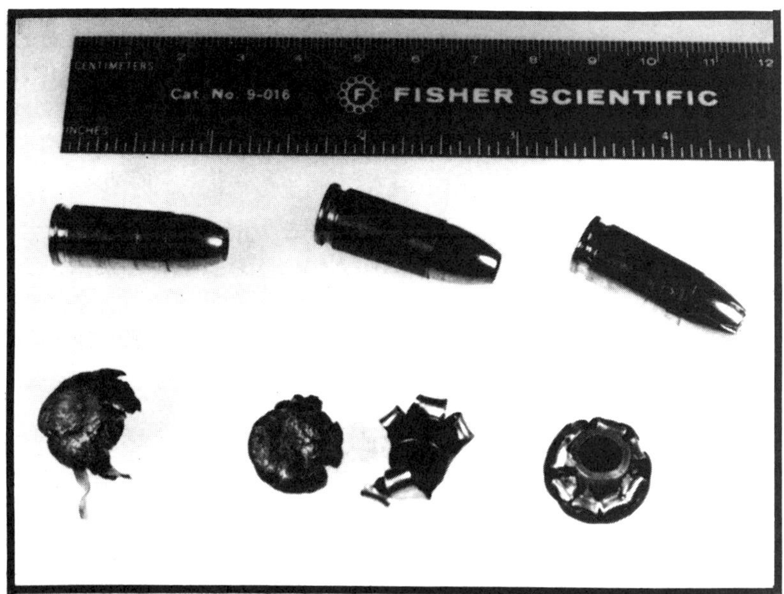

Left to right: The Federal 9mm 115-grain JHP, the CCI Blazer 115-grain JHP, and the Winchester Silvertip 115-grain JHP. All expand very well when fired into water.

A special problem is that of the person who has only a small caliber for defense. Not everyone can afford the several hundreds of dollars that some handguns cost. Unfortunately, the people who need protection the most are probably the ones who live in the worst neighborhoods because they're on the tightest budgets, raising their families on very modest salaries. If you're in that category, and you have a handgun you picked up second-hand, you might have a small-caliber weapon that many would consider too small for the purpose.

You have to make do with what you have. One way is to get high-performance ammunition for it. In this regard, the picture is getting better every day. Winchester makes a high-performance JHP with a ball-bearing in the nose for the .25 ACP. This strange little bullet travels too slowly for reliable expansion using normal technology, and the ball-bearing helps promote expansion at the slower velocity.

Expanding loads are available for the other small calibers. Winchester makes Silvertips in calibers .32 ACP and .380 ACP. The Glaser Safety Slug is a special load that is very expensive per cartridge, but delivers very high performance. The Glaser slug is a copper jacket filled with tiny shot suspended in an oily liquid. The jacket's nose is covered by a plastic cap, which aids feeding in auto pistols. Upon impact, the hollow jacket ruptures, releasing the tiny balls into the target. This makes a worse wound than most hollow-points. Glasers come in six-packs, at a cost of ten to fifteen dollars per six-pack. This is costly, but affordable, since Glasers are not practice ammo. If ever you have to use one for real, you'll be glad you have them.

Let's wind this up with a couple of valuable points:

In some instances, penetration is more important than expansion. In hot climates where people dress lightly, you don't have to worry about a heavy coat absorbing some of the bullet's power. In cold climates, very heavy clothing can interfere with the penetration of the JHPs. This depends on a lot of factors, such as bullet weight and velocity, but a general rule is to use a cartridge with a heavier bullet to be sure, even though it travels at less velocity.

The other point is that tactics are more important than hardware. Believe it, and don't worry if your gun is a pip-squeak caliber that barely suffices for an angry dog. Worry instead about being behind cover, so that your opponent's bullets won't hit you, whatever weapon he's using.

LEARNING TO SHOOT

If you already know how to shoot, you might be tempted to skip this chapter. Don't. The reason is that you might have learned your shooting in situations that taught you the wrong habits for survival. If you've learned by plinking, or hunting, this won't prepare you to fight for your life. This chapter will start you on learning to shoot to win close encounters of the worst kind. You'll learn some concrete tips on shooting in a way that's different from what you've been doing.

You'll learn some quick drills that will help in a tense situation. Drawing and firing quickly when confronted by an attacker is one drill. Clearing a jammed weapon is another. They are part of a set of basic "building blocks" of tactics that you'll need to win.

Let's start with how to aim the weapon, be it rifle, pistol, or shotgun. "Sight" would be the wrong word for close-in defensive shooting. You don't use the sights close up. The exact distance depends on the situation, but you should not need to use the sights to hit a man-size target at twenty feet or closer. In a defensive situation, the light will probably be too dim to let you see the sights, anyway.

STARTING WITH DRY PRACTICE

First make sure that the weapon's empty. Practice bringing it up to eye level and looking over the barrel to line it up with your target. What target? You can tape a silhouette to the wall of your room. This necessary first step is to get the "feel" of the weapon, and will be "dry fire" only. Don't be in a hurry to use live ammo. Why not?

Americans regularly go out to the range and burn up box after box of ammunition. This is natural, as this is one of the wealthiest countries in the world. It isn't necessary to burn up so much ammo to learn to shoot, and citizens of other countries learn and maintain their shooting skills with a lot less ammo burning. The armed forces have techniques of training recruits, using "dry fire" that don't waste ammo.

Keep practicing bringing the weapon up to eye level while keeping your eyes on the target. Keep your eyes on the target, not the sights. You may have been told that the key to quick and accurate shooting is to watch the front sight. This is true in competition, where the targets can't shoot back. On the street, your opponent may be drawing a gun, or he may have an accomplice, which is why you must keep your eyes focused out there, where the threat is.

Use one hand or two? With a shoulder weapon, you'll usually need two. You'll also find that using both hands helps steady the weapon if it's a pistol. However, don't learn to depend on having both hands free to hold the handgun. It'll take you longer to learn, but it's better to practice with one hand. The only reason firearms instructors teach their students to use both hands on the pistol is because this gets results faster. Out on the street, however, even police officers often find that they don't have both hands free if they need to open fire.

If you're locked in to using use both hands on the weapon, you'll find yourself caught short in close encounters of the worst kind.

Practice your trigger pull. Although in a gunfight you'll be pulling the trigger very quickly, you need to make sure that you don't jerk the gun when you do. This is where only dry fire can help, as the blast and recoil of shooting a live round masks trigger jerk.

If you find that the weapon dips down when you pull the trigger, slow down. Practice holding it on target and squeezing the trigger slowly so that the muzzle doesn't dip when the trigger "breaks." You may need several sessions practicing this alone, until you get it right.

Later, when you're firing live ammo, you'll possibly find yourself shooting low. If this happens, stop and repeat the empty-gun trigger exercises. This is a problem that many people find persists, even after they become experienced shots.

When you get tired, stop and take a break. Think about what you've done, and mentally rehearse it again and again. When you feel rested, stand up and continue. Resist the temptation to try for speed. Take your time. Concentrate on bringing the gun up smoothly and lining it up on target without overshooting and wasting motion. Do this slowly, because getting it right is more important than saving a fraction of a second.

Think about this point. If you raise the weapon as fast as you can in a real situation, rushing yourself and then missing, it'll take you the better part of a second to correct. You'll be under even more pressure, and in an even greater hurry. This will increase your chances of missing even more. In a gunfight, it's not the first shot fired that counts; it's the first one that hits.

When you raise your weapon, learn to slow down during the last part of the arc, to avoid raising the muzzle beyond horizontal. If you bring the gun up too far, you'll have to come down, and this will take time.

You should be familiar enough with your weapon that you don't have to look at it when you bring it up. Your finger should find the trigger naturally. If you keep a pistol in a pocket or holster, don't ever look at it while drawing. Your hand should find it as easily as it finds the zipper on your pants, without fumbling or hesitating. A fumble costs time.

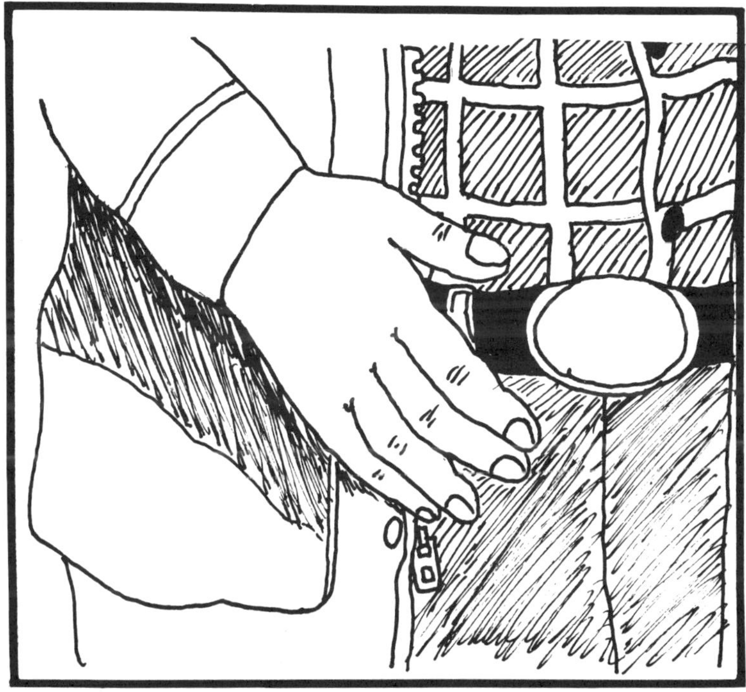

If you intend to carry your pistol under a jacket, practice drawing it with the jacket on. Practice brushing the jacket aside far enough to clear the weapon, or you'll lose valuable time if ever you have to draw for real!

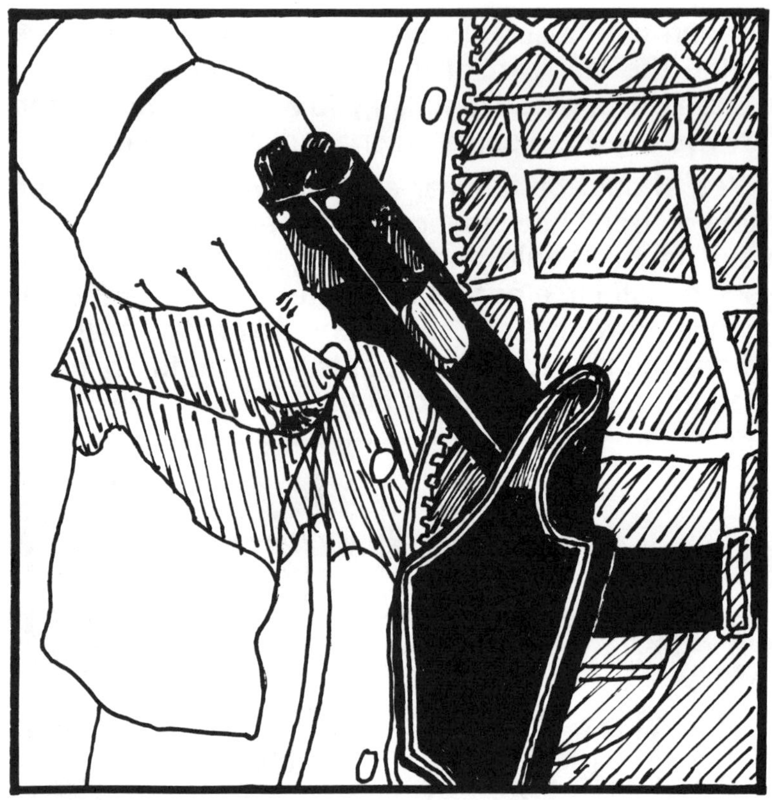

One tip to help you is to keep the holster in the same place to avoid confusion. Once you decide where you want it, always keep it there. That way, you'll always put your hand in the same place and your fingers will naturally close on the butt without searching. This also applies to reaching for extra ammo and to reholstering. You should not have to take your eyes off the scene in front of you to do these. If you can't manage this now, practice until you can.

A similar process works for a shoulder weapon. Always pick it up in the same way. You need to build muscle memory so that you'll bring the weapon up automatically, without having to decide where to place your hands.

If you have an auto pistol with an external safety, always leave it either on "ON" or "OFF." Experienced shooters disagree on whether the best practice is to keep it one way or the other, but there's no disagreement that you should be consistent. If you leave the safety "OFF" when practicing, then put it "ON" when you go out on the street, you're going to hesitate while you try to remember which way you left it. This hesitation can get you killed if an opponent opens fire while you're still trying to decide about the safety. You'll be *dead wrong.*

You're probably best off not keeping an external safety "ON." If you have a weapon that goes "cocked and locked," so that you must keep the safety "ON" to prevent an accidental discharge, you'd be better off with another weapon. It's too dangerous to carry with you.

In a real-life crisis, not having to release a manual safety means that there's one less thing to remember and do. When your life's on the line, you need to cut your reaction time as much as you can, and anything that slows you down is undesirable. Of course, an expert competitive shooter can draw a single-action pistol, flick the safety off, and fire faster than you or I can think about it. This speed takes hundreds or even thousands of hours of practice to attain, and most people, including police officers, don't have the time for it.

This is why police for decades have favored the double-action revolver over the many auto pistols on the market. To fire a D.A. revolver, all you need to do is to pull the trigger. An internal mechanism prevents accidental firings when the hammer is down and the finger is off the trigger. Pulling the trigger cocks the hammer and pulls a hammer block bar out of the way. Another type of double-action mechanism raises a "transfer bar" to transfer the hammer's impact to the firing pin when the trigger is pulled back.

The new double-action autos with internal safeties also have this method of operation. All the shooter needs to do is pull the trigger. Internal safeties keep the weapon from firing accidentally, even if dropped.

Practice drawing and clicking your weapon at the target at least fifty times per day for at least a week. You can do this before leaving for work, or after you come home. If you have the time, a hundred times per day is even better.

Don't just practice from a standing position. Practice firing from behind cover, and from sitting, crouching, and prone positions. Find out how awkward it can be to draw a weapon while prone, and decide what you're going to do if ever the situation demands that you go prone to return fire.

Also practice drawing and firing from the quarter-hip position. This is sometimes called "hip-shooting," and is valuable close-up. In some face to face confrontations, you'll need to open fire as soon as your weapon's out and lined up. You won't be able to bring it up to eye level because the opponent's too close. In such a case put out the other arm, as if to deflect the opponent's weapon, and fire as soon as you feel your weapon's lined up.

Always stop when you get tired, but resume later. Also practice late at night, when you're tired. This will give you the feel of gun handling when you are not at your best. This is necessary because muggers and intruders don't make appointments with you.

If you should wake up during the night, try for a practice session right then. Again, make sure the weapon is empty.

RELOADING

Practice loading and unloading your weapon. You can do this safely at home with a revolver or auto pistol. With a revolver, carefully load the cylinder with fired cases first. With an auto pistol, use empty magazines.

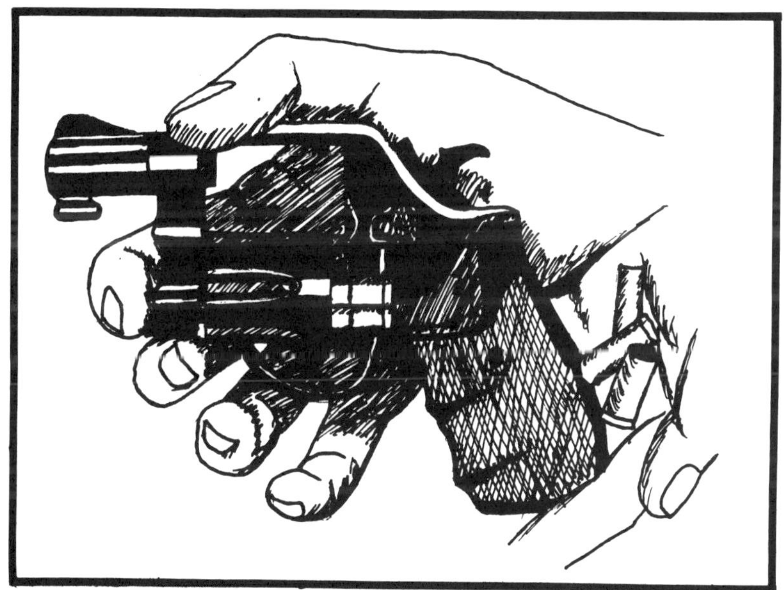

When unloading a revolver, always hold it muzzle-up, so that gravity helps you eject the empties from the chambers. If you catch them in the palm of your hand, you'll slow yourself down. Let the empties drop!

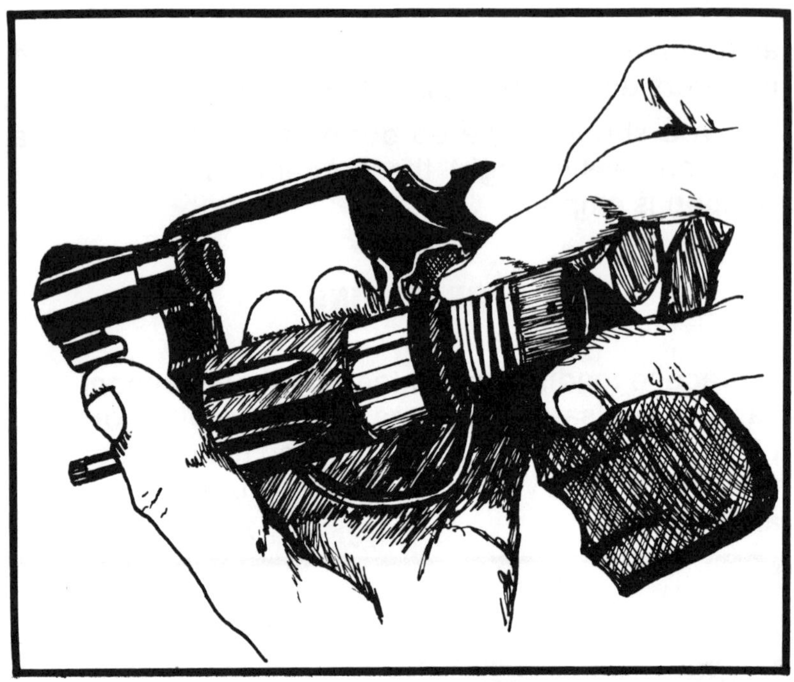

Practice reloading using a speedloader. This rams six fresh shells at a time into the cylinder. Also practice loading with "loose change," shells from your pocket, because you may not always have a speedloader available.

LIVE FIRE

When you feel ready to fire ammunition, go out to an isolated place where you can set up some large cardboard targets at a range of thirty feet or less. Start firing from close in.

At six feet from your target, raise your weapon and fire two shots. Lower it half-way, and scan your target. Resist the temptation to open up on your target with everything you have, emptying your weapon in one joyous burst of fire. You might do this once or twice, just to get it out of your system, but you're better off practicing in bursts of two shots.

The reason is that you can't ever assume that you'll have only one enemy. It's tempting to wipe out an opponent in one annihilating burst of gunfire, but this leaves nothing for possible accomplices.

Let's break off here and discuss habits. Good shooting for survival is building and practicing good shooting habits. You must learn to draw, bring your weapon up, line it up, and squeeze off two shots by habit, without having to think about each step. Compare this with tying your shoelaces. You do it automatically, without conscious thought. Once you make the decision to put on your shoes and tie the laces, you do it without further deliberation. Driving a car works the same way. When you started, you had to think about every move. Now you can drive and carry on a conversation at the same time.

Training yourself to shoot this way doesn't mean that you're programming yourself to be a killer or to open fire indiscriminately. Not at all. You're actually programming shooting into conditioned reflexes, so that you leave your mind free to make the important decisions, such as whether or not you're justified in shooting.

Along with building good shooting habits, you must also avoid starting bad ones. "Bad" in this case means bad for your purpose. If you're a target shooter, you may have become used to extracting your fired shells carefully and putting them in your pocket or into a bag. Some rifle shooters even put their empties back into the box. There's no time to do this in a shoot-out, because the delay can get you killed. Dumping your fired cases onto the ground gets them dirty, but so what? It's better having to clean your cases than to clean up blood — your blood.

The same goes for empty magazines, if you're firing an auto pistol. Don't take the empty magazine carefully out of the weapon and place it in your pocket. You can't afford the split-second it takes in a gunfight. Let it drop. Of course, this risks damage to the magazine, but buy a couple of extras and use them only for practice.

Watch yourself for other bad habits:

Looking to see where your fired cases have fallen, if you're shooting an auto pistol.

Pausing after each shot to peer at the target, looking for the hole.

Looking at your weapon to confirm that the safety's "OFF."

This is where practicing with a friend can help. You can monitor each other for bad habits.

Continue firing at short ranges until you're satisfied that you can hit the target every time, and hit quickly. Gradually open up the range to about thirty feet. This is likely to be the maximum range at which you'll ever have to shoot to save your life. When you can shoot well at all ranges up to thirty feet, you're ready for some low light practice.

LOW LIGHT SHOOTING

Most gunfights take place in poor light. The reason is that the street maggots come out at night.

Start with dry fire again. Practice drawing and firing an empty gun to check yourself for smooth operation. When you only have the light from the next room, or street lights, you can't look to see what you're doing. If you can't find your holstered weapon in the dark, shame on you!

Never, never, use a flashlight as an aiming aid. This can get you killed. Ignore all of the "flashlight shooting positions" devised by people who named them after themselves. A light draws fire, and gives your enemy a beautiful target while he can stay in the shadows. Even if you hold the light out away from yourself, spilling light on a nearby wall can silhouette you.

Practice when it's so dark that you can barely see your weapon and the target. The trick to hitting in low light is shooting by feel. The technical term for this is "kinesthetic sense." This is the feel of knowing where the different parts of your body are without looking. After some practice in good light you'll find that you can close your eyes, draw, and line up the weapon fairly accurately. Check yourself a few times to see how well you can do this, and if you're satisfied, practice in bad light.

Go out to the boonies again for another practice session, but this time in the early morning or evening, when the light is poor. Evening is best, because you won't be rushed by the rising sun.

If it's inky black, you can always supply some light with a flashlight or your car's headlights. Don't ever hold a flashlight in your hand while shooting, though. This is another bad habit that can cost you your life.

You'll find that your accuracy falls off in poor light. You also may find that your shots drift up or down. Some firearms instructors claim that their students tend to shoot low or high in poor light, but this probably has more to do with the techniques taught than with any natural tendency.

USING THE SIGHTS

You may want to practice long-range shooting, too. This can be essential if you live in a rural area.

The basic technique is to keep your eyes on the target, and bring the weapon up so that the sights come between your eyes and the target. This isn't just another way of describing it. It shows a different way of thinking. In target shooting, you place your eyes behind the sights and look for the target. In shooting to survive, you dare not take your eyes off your adversary, and you bring the sights up while scanning the target carefully. When the sights are lined up, you don't take your eyes off the target. You just shift focus, letting the target blur for a second while you give the sight alignment a quick final check, and fire.

With a shoulder weapon, long-range shooting is also deliberate shooting. If you've got a scope-sighted rifle, you'll want to take cover and to use a rest for your weapon. Often, you can use your cover for a rest, being careful not to let yourself become silhouetted against a light background.

LEARNING YOUR LIMITS

The most important thing you'll do in your practice sessions is to learn your limits. You'll find what is the farthest range you can draw and hit a man-size target without deliberate aim. You'll learn your reaction time. It's important to know your limits for two critical reasons:

1. You can discover where you need improvement.
2. You will find out what you can't do, and this will help you to plan realistic tactics. For example, if you know you can't hit accurately without using the sights at thirty feet, you'll know not even to try in a real gunfight.

Once you've learned your limits in this first-stage training program, you can try yourself at harder tasks. The first is the "stress test." Sprint one hundred yards to the target, draw, and fire two shots from twenty feet. Did you hit, or were your hands shaking? Don't be surprised if you missed with both shots. Let's see why, and what this has to do with real life.

We've already discussed some of the effects of fear. The immediate effects are an increased heartbeat, rapid respiration, muscular tension, and even tremors. In some extreme cases, people lose bowel and bladder control from extreme fear. This is why even good shots often miss in a gunfight. While it's impossible to induce artificially all of the effects of extreme fear, we can bring on some of them by running.

Practice regularly shooting a few rounds after running one or two hundred yards. You'll find that you quickly steady down, and hit your targets consistently.

Do you drink alcohol? If so, either learn to abstain or learn to handle a weapon with a few drinks in you. This is against all conventional advice, but it's valid. It's fine for someone to moralize and say self-righteously that you should not drink and carry a weapon, but the real world isn't that way. Even police officers "stop off" for a few drinks after work, and many carry off-duty guns.

Of course, there are other reasons for not drinking alcohol in certain circumstances. If you have to drive, you'd better be sober. However, suppose you have a few drinks at home, before going to bed. An intruder tries to force his way in. What can you do? Ask him to come back after the alcohol is out of your system?

A lot depends on the individual. There's no doubt that alcohol incapacitates, but this varies with different people. Some people can drink moderately and drive for years without a ticket or an accident. This isn't to encourage you to drink and drive, but to advise you to know your limits.

Unless you decide here and now to give up drinking, try shooting live ammo while under the influence. This doesn't mean that you should drink until you're incapacitated, but only one or two, a reasonable and customary amount. Have a friend drive you out to the boonies and drive you home, for safety's sake.

If you're like most people, you'll find that alcohol doesn't impair your marksmanship. It can impair your judgment, and this is much harder to detect. This is the greater danger, because many wrongful deaths involve alcohol. Under the influence, some people become argumentative and combative, and reach for a weapon. If you find alcohol impairing your judgment, try to avoid drinking when there's a weapon within reach.

You also need to test your limits in a confrontation. Buy a rubber knife, and ask a friend to help you. Have him stand ten feet away and come for you with the knife. If you have a stopwatch, time him. You'll be surprised to find that an adult male can walk ten feet in about a second and one-half.

With an empty gun in your holster, ask him to charge you. Find out for yourself how closely you can allow an attacker armed with a knife to approach before you're in deadly danger. Try this exercise again while wearing a jacket and with your holstered weapon under the jacket. By trial and error, determine how far away he must be before you feel safe.

MALFUNCTIONS

Both revolvers and auto pistols can malfunction. It's dangerous to generalize, because there are many exceptions, but we can lay down some rules of thumb:

Revolvers have more delicate mechanisms, and are more open to the entry of dirt. They're more likely to jam because of dirt. A jam in a revolver is harder to clear than one in an auto pistol.

A high primer will jam the cylinder if you don't see it and try to close the cylinder. The only way to clear this is to remove and discard the cartridge.

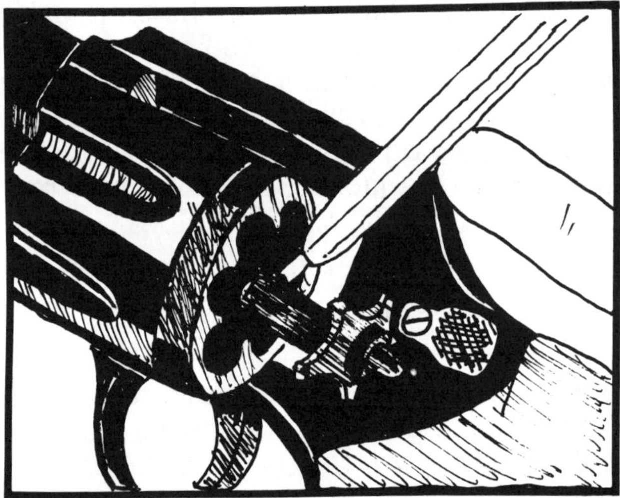

Before loading your revolver, check for dirt under the extractor star. A small amount of dirt or grit here can jam the cylinder. The only cure is to clean out the dirt.

Auto pistols are sensitive to ammunition power and to damaged magazine lips. Malfunctions will most likely occur in feeding.

With auto pistols, there's an all-purpose jam-clearing drill, called "TAP-RACK-BANG." This usually puts the weapon back in action in a second or two. The first step is to "TAP" the magazine on the underside, because it may not be seated all the way. There also might be a slight hold-up in the feeding, caused by a piece of dirt in the magazine. A tap will usually clear this up.

This is a stovepipe jam, with a fired shell half-way out of the ejection port. Racking the slide while sweeping the empty away with the edge of the hand will clear this.

The next step is to "RACK" the slide. This means to grab it by the front, keeping fingers away from the muzzle, and push the slide back sharply. By sweeping the hand over the slide as you do this, you will clear any stovepipe jams.

Finally, you pull the trigger, "BANG." If this doesn't clear it, you have to take another look. Practice going for cover when you do your malfunction-clearing drills.

This is a "cocked round," one that's jumped out of the magazine a bit too hard and jammed on the side of the chamber. A similar malfunction is the "double-feed," which has two cartridges trying to get into the chamber at the same time. A quick way to clear this is to turn the pistol upside-down and work the slide once by hand. If this doesn't work, you need to lock the slide back, withdraw the magazine enough to break the engagement of the cocked round, shake out the loose cartridges, tap the magazine home, and let the slide close.

MAINTAINING

Learning to shoot can be a rewarding experience. It can also be fun. However, don't assume that once you've taught yourself, you don't have to do anything else. Shooting is a psychomotor skill that you have to maintain with regular practice. At least go through a session of dry practice at home once a week. Fire live ammo out on the range once a month. Good luck and good shooting.

GUNFIGHTING: MYTH AND REALITY

There are many myths about gunfighting, many of them created and spread by the movies and TV. This happens because the portrayals have been written and enacted by people who have never been in a gunfight and probably have never seen a real one. The script writers are usually trying for dramatic impact rather than realism.

Let's cover these myths quickly:

1. The participants almost never face each other with holstered guns, "High Noon" style.
2. Most shots miss, not surprising considering the dim light and the urgency.
3. Gunfights aren't usually long battles. They're over in a few seconds, after a quick exchange of shots.
4. People who get shot don't fall down instantly, as we see on TV. They often take a while to collapse, particularly if they've been hit in a non-vital area.

5. There's no time for careful aim, which makes it impossible to "shoot to wound" or "shoot to kill." You must simply shoot to hit.
6. Nobody "fans" his gun, except in the movies.
7. The winner doesn't simply reholster his gun and walk triumphantly into the sunset. Unless the shoot-out took place in a secluded area, and the winner "walks away," there will be complications from the police.

With the myths out of the way, let's look at some basic tactical principles:

1. The main idea is your survival. A gunfight is not a suicide mission nor is it a *macho* trip. Don't be afraid to seek cover because you think it's cowardly or unmanly.
2. Cover and concealment are good for you and bad for your enemy. Try to arrange things so that you have cover and he's left in the open.
3. Visibility should favor you. It's best if you can see him clearly to aim but he can't see you. Keep to the shadows.
4. Try for surprise. Sometimes your enemy has it on his side, as in a robbery. If you can regain the initiative and surprise him, you may gain a precious second before he reacts.
5. Speed counts. Do what you have to, and do it fast. Your moves should already be planned. If the situation changes, don't stall. Decide and act now. What might have been a good move seconds ago could be a bad move now, so don't waste time.

6. Accuracy's important, too. Make your first shot count. For example, if you're ambushing an intruder, be sure you get him with the first burst. Missing means warning him and losing the initiative.
7. Always fire bursts of two. Don't wait between shots.
8. Avoid getting caught with an empty gun. Your enemy may rush you.

Special situations call for special measures, but these are the basics. The theme and the purpose are to do what you can to score hits while protecting yourself.

TARGET SHOOTING AND COMBAT MATCHES

Most people who learn to shoot in this country learn in a way that's more suitable for the target range than for a fight for life. The only good point about this practice is that it's possible to learn about the care and feeding of weapons this way. You learn the basics of loading and unloading the weapon. You also learn to clean it. You'll surely pick up some rules for safe gun handling on the range. You can also pick up some bad habits and misleading knowledge.

The reason is that there's a vast difference between shooting for score and shooting for survival. When you shoot to live you have no time to aim properly or to use breath and trigger control. You'll be flushed and excited. There won't be time to hold your breath while you *squeeze* the trigger. You'll be doing well if you're still breathing.

You'll probably be pointing, not aiming, your weapon, and pulling the trigger as quickly as you can. You target-shooting skills won't count, and if you take an extra second to check your sight picture it may cost you your life.

In defensive shooting, tactics are far more important than marksmanship. Being able to place five shots in a small circle at fifty yards won't be very relevant when you're trying to stop an enemy five feet away. Likewise, taking several seconds to "frame" your shot wastes time you can't afford when you're racing against a deadly enemy instead of a stopwatch.

COMBAT MATCHES

This type of competition pretends to simulate real-life shooting against other human beings. Actually, the ideas and methods you learn at combat or practical matches can be very misleading.

Typically, matches are held in bright daylight, although a few shooting clubs have night shoots. The range officer announces the course of fire, the rules, and the points needed to win. Targets are usually ten to fifty yards away, and never, never shoot back at you. If you don't do well, the penalty is losing points, not being shot to death. The winner doesn't get arrested for having an illegal weapon or for manslaughter.

If you ever have to defend yourself in real life, it'll probably come down like this:

Your assailants will be much closer, probably within touching distance. The light will be poor, and nobody will make an appointment with you in advance. There will be no range officer to referee the match. You'll be taken by surprise, and in circumstances that you would not have chosen if you'd had the choice.

EQUIPMENT

You can also pick up some very misleading ideas about equipment. Some competitors think that the equipment that wins matches is the best to win on the street, too. It's surprising that they believe that a custom-built gun with extended slide and sights is the best for a real-life deadly contest. You'll also see speed rigs, holsters designed for very quick draw, and which are not practical on the street.

Often, you'll hear that the Government Model in .45 ACP is the best handgun of all. You'll hear all sorts of claims about its stopping power and general suitability for combat. You might be tempted to buy one after hearing these claims. Don't be in too much of a hurry.

Service veterans were not very impressed with it. They found it hard to shoot, and often preferred the foreign hardware better. This is why many American veterans returned from WW II with German Lugers and P-38s. Japanese pistols were mediocre, but the German hardware clearly outclassed our own.

It's true that the Government .45 makes a good showing in combat matches, but these are not real-life gunfights. The contestants are usually expert shots who would do well with most handguns.

Most of the weapons fired by the winners are not true out-of-the-box weapons, but expensively reworked versions. Some contestants have weapons with a total value of fifteen hundred dollars or more. This isn't exactly a run of the mill defensive weapon. It bears as much relationship to the gun you're likely to own as an Indianapolis race car does to the one sitting in your carport.

Unfortunately, the weapon doesn't function very well without many expensive modifications. Ask any ex-GI and ask any competitor.

Although the Government .45 is a classic, like the DC-3, it's obsolete, having been designed during the first decade of this century. Many later and better designs are available today.

WHAT WORKS ON THE STREET

Match hardware and tactics aren't worth anything when your life is on the line. What works in the sterile and hygienic atmosphere of competitive shooting has nothing to do with what you need to know and use out where it counts, on the hot asphalt. You need different equipment and a different set of tactics. That's what this book is all about.

GUNS AND TACTICS

Let's start by saying that hardware and tactics are inter-related. You have to know that they're not isolated subjects, and understand how they go together. Tactics are the main message of this book, because good tactics can pull you out of a bad situation, and bad tactics can get you hurt or killed.

Because hardware and tactics go together, let's look at the problems of owning and carrying a gun. Where do you keep it? In some situations that answer is obvious; home in bed you keep it close at hand, although there may be some ifs, ands, and buts. What about the householder who regularly has nightmares? Is it safe for him to place a weapon where he can reach it while asleep? What about sleepwalkers? They, too, have a right to defend themselves, but they have a special problem.

What about the family with children? Is it possible to leave a loaded weapon where they can reach it? Is it advisable to lock the weapon up every morning?

Each person has to answer these questions. Each situation is different. The parent with teenagers can handle the problem differently than one with toddlers. The person with persistent nightmares might seek medical help.

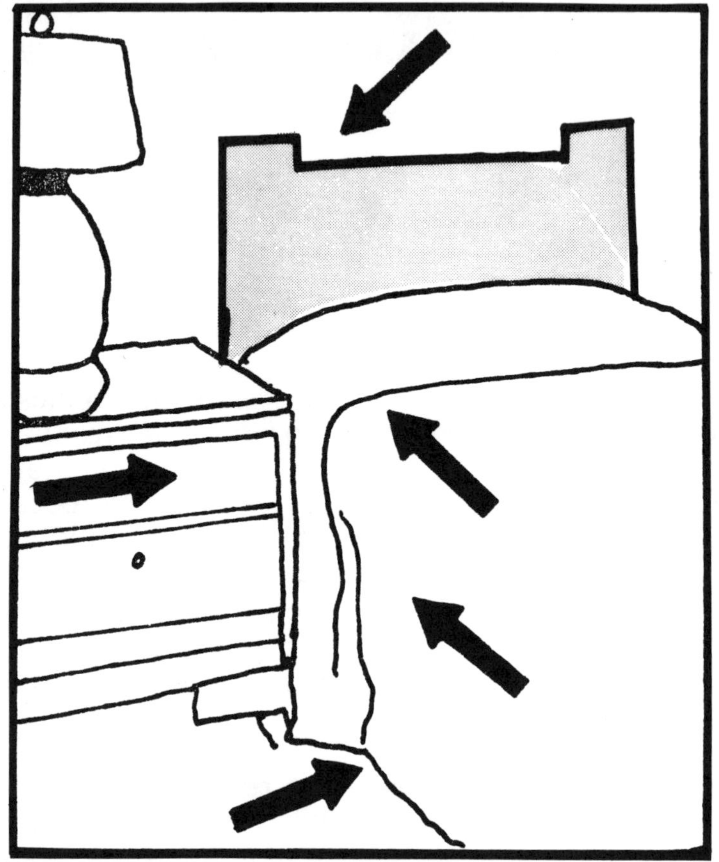

There are several places to keep a weapon in the bedroom. Under the pillow is okay, but not if you tumble around a lot. A holster behind the headboard is another possibility. Keeping it on the floor under the bed is probably the best place, because any size weapon will fit, and it can't ever fall.

There are special techniques available for householders with children. One is constant carry, keeping the weapon on your person and under your control at all times. This can be a problem if it's a large weapon. The other is to keep only the ammunition on you. If you decide to keep an auto pistol for protection, carry the magazine with you. If your weapon is a revolver, carrying a speedloader in your pocket will allow you to leave the empty gun within reach of children too young to understand gun safety. It's far more difficult with a rifle or shotgun, because loading can be very slow. A .22 caliber rifle with a magazine loading system will work, but loading a shotgun's tubular magazine takes precious seconds and makes noise.

A shoulder holster is workable if you wear a jacket. The best kind for concealment are those which carry the handgun somewhat muzzle-high, which blends it best into the body's contours.

Some home defense situations are so hazardous that the householder might decide to carry the weapon on the person at all times, or at least to park it within reach. It can be troublesome to carry a shotgun around with every step you take, and if you live in this sort of area you might consider moving out, whatever the cost.

A belt holster will do very well for many purposes, and is even concealable under a heavy jacket or coat. However, if you're thinking of needing your pistol while riding in a car, also think of how you're going to draw it.

If the weapon is a handgun, is a holster advisable? We've already seen that holsters are not always the answer. The main purpose of a holster, frankly, is to protect clothing. Pockets are not made to carry heavy metal objects. Holsters available today are both well-made and even stylish. Some leather ones are very expensive. The nylon ones are much less costly, as little as ten dollars.

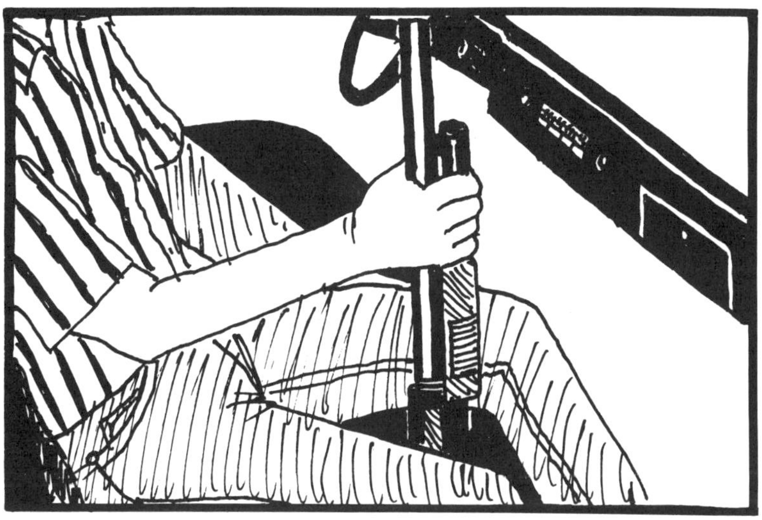

The same for a shoulder weapon. If you need to ride shotgun in a car, you'll find this between-the-knees carry very comfortable. However, it's very slow for getting the gun into action. If you have to leave the car quickly, you'll only get it tangled in your legs.

Tucking the pistol in your belt or your pocket also isn't the best way for a fast draw. If you're thinking of this, remember that many holsters are designed for this. However, how often do you really need a quick draw? Quick draw is a reaction to surprise, but if you use good tactics you can avoid being surprised. At home, if you keep the doors and windows locked, nobody can surprise you. Outside, if you feel that you're going into a bad situation, the quickest draw is to have the pistol already in your hand.

An ankle holster is good for wearing a handgun when you can't wear it on your belt or under your armpit. However, understand that it's slow on the draw. Another point is that, for maximum concealment, the gun's barrel should be on a diagonal, blending the weapon with the shape of your calf. If the barrel is straight up-and-down, the butt will stick out too far.

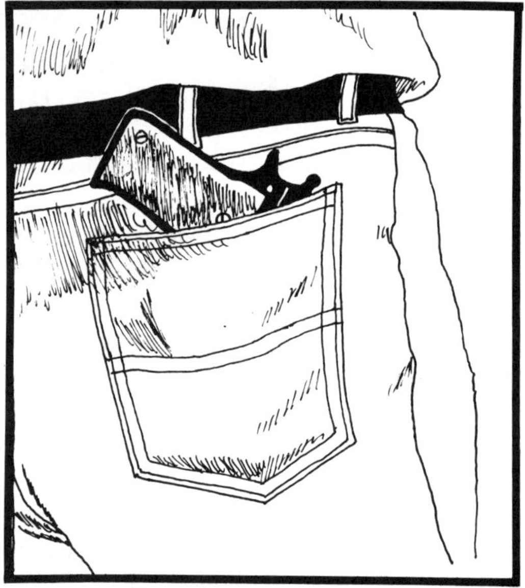

The pocket carry will do for many situations. Remember that it's only an expedient with a large handgun, because the weapon will quickly wear holes in your clothing. Sitting down with a handgun in your back pocket will do this very quickly.

Walking around with a pistol in your hand might attract unwanted attention, so you have to work your way around this. One is to keep your hand and gun in your coat pocket. However, if you stalk around this way, giving everyone you meet dirty looks, you'll give the impression of a movie gangster. If you can keep both hands in your pockets and act casual, you may get away with it. A street-smart mugger will always look to see where your hands are. He won't let you take your hands out of your pockets. You may feel something pressed into your back, or he'll pop out from a corner or doorway with drawn gun, and that will be it.

A better way is to carry it in something that looks natural, something that belongs. Carrying it in a paper bag in your hand is natural. Grip it loosely so that the outline doesn't show. A larger weapon may fit in a grocery bag. The container has to fit in with the locale. A violin case or a golf bag look out of place in the ghetto. A paper-wrapped package would not.

SHOOT OR DON'T SHOOT?

Another basic decision to make is whether you shoot or not. You may find using the gun as a club better in a few situations.

The first reason is the danger to bystanders from shots fired. If you miss, or if the bullets go through your attacker, they can injure others.

The second reason is that a handgun, whatever the caliber, is a marginal weapon. Your attacker may not go down quickly enough if you shoot him, and might pump a shot into you as he succumbs. If he's within reach you might find it quicker to club him in the head, as hard as you can.

Finally, in locales such as New York, if you're carrying the weapon illegally, opening fire is truly the last resort. Shots will attract police officers, and you'll be in as much trouble as the suspect. Opening fire is only for when there's no other way.

If you decide to use your handgun as a weapon, there's a right way to do it, and several wrong ways.

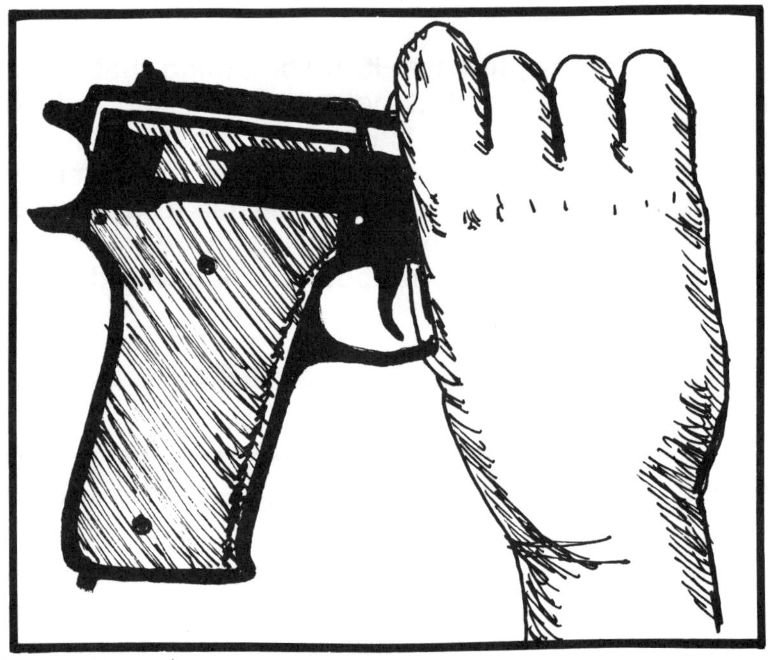

Don't grip it this way, hoping to rake him with the rear sight as you slug him. This is amateurish. It's also slow. You'll have to shift your weapon in your hand after you draw it. Holding it the other way, to strike him with the butt, is also slow, and very poor tactics. The adversary can grab the weapon by the grip, insert his finger into the trigger guard, and shoot you for having the barrel so conveniently pointing at you.

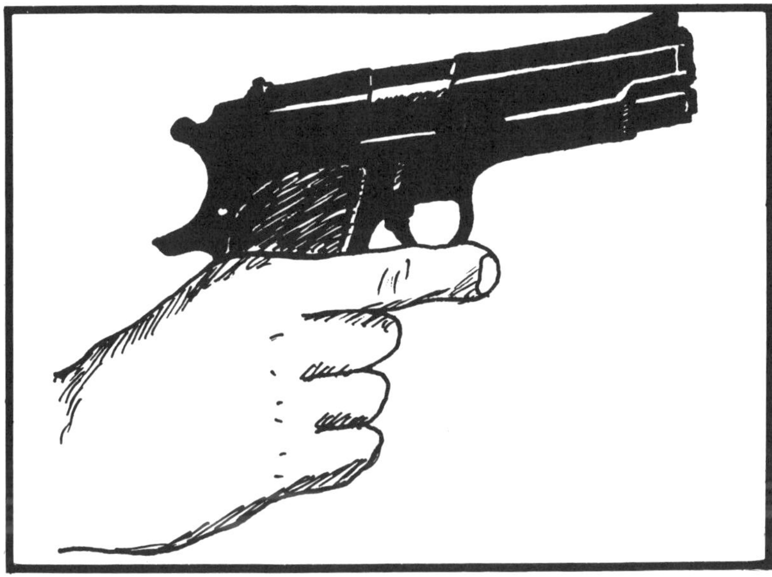

This is a far better way. You strike with the front of the slide, and retain a firm grip on the weapon. If you have to, you can quickly trigger the weapon.

TACTICS ARE ESSENTIAL

Knowing how to use your weapon effectively is more than knowing how to load and unload it, and where to find the trigger. It also includes good tactics. Learning to shoot is an essential first step. Learning how to fight with a firearm is next.

PRE-PROGRAMMED DECISIONS: THE MENTAL TRIGGERS FOR ACTION

When you come face to face with a criminal, it's too late to start planning. You should have your basic decisions already made, and the on-the-spot thinking you do should be on the basis of pre-programmed decisions. In one sense, you've already made the first decision, you'll resist if possible. Other decisions you should have made are:

- Cover: What cover will you use?
- Warning: Should you give a verbal warning, or just open fire?
- Others: Are you concerned about others' safety, or are you alone with the criminal?

There are many other questions to answer, but the answers shouldn't be difficult. You ought to think of every one as:

"If this, then..."

This is a pre-programmed decision. You don't agonize over questions, or try to make value judgments. You've already done that. You observe and evaluate the situation, and take the appropriate action.

Another term for a pre-programmed decision is mental trigger. You decide what you're going to do if something happens. If it does, you react.

Deciding on your tactics is equally quick, although not that simple. You start with an inventory of tactical building blocks which we'll cover in various chapters in this book. You then apply the ones which fit the situation.

PRACTICAL GUNFIGHTING TACTICS

Tactics will make it or break it. Along with learning to operate your weapon effectively, you need to know how to make the most of the tactical situation.

AVOID TUBE TRAINING

Tube training is the term used for learning from TV cop shows. As we've already noted, many myths, including bad tactics, are spread by TV script writers and TV actors. Some of these tactics can quickly get you killed.

ALERTNESS

Unless you keep mentally alert you can wind up in very serious trouble. It's very much like driving a car. Keeping alert, aware of traffic, and practicing defensive driving will help keep you alive.

There have been several gimmicky color code systems used to describe states of alertness. These are unnecessary if you understand the basic facts.

THE SPACE-TIME CUSHION

This is fundamental to success in an armed encounter. Space translates directly into time, and vice-versa, in many encounters. An attacker needs time to travel across a certain amount of space to reach you. Keeping space between you and an opponent gives you time. Space protects you even though a bullet can cross that space in an insignificant amount of time. The farther you are from an attacker, the more time he needs to aim.

COVER

This means protection from bullets. You can find cover behind a wall or a piece of furniture. You can also use a telephone pole, tree, car, or stone wall for cover.

The most important thing to keep in mind about cover is that it's relative. What offers good cover against one type of weapon won't help much against a more powerful one. For example, most interior walls will stop a B-B, and it'll stop number eight bird-shot, if fired at thirty feet or more, but little else. Wall studs will stop many pistol bullets, but they're spaced a foot or more apart in a wall. It's even worse in a house trailer or a mobile home. Their walls are made of hefty cardboard and even less resistant to penetration.

Double-ought buckshot blasts through an interior wall. Keep this in mind when considering a weapon for home defense.

A .22 Long Rifle bullet goes through an interior wall like a hot knife through butter.

Cars, mailboxes, and other objects commonly found outdoors offer varying protection against gunfire. A thick tree, large enough to conceal you completely, will stop many rifle bullets and practically any handgun bullet fired at it. The cover a car provides varies with the part of the car you're using.

This is the wrong way to use a part of the car that will stop bullets effectively. Exposing your upper body is foolish, and doesn't give you any tactical advantages.

This is better. Keep most of your body right behind the engine and tires, and expose only what you need to for aiming.

Always keep in mind what your opponent can see. In this case, you're letting him have a clear shot at your legs and feet.

You can't always get a clear shot from right behind the engine. The rear of a vehicle will provide cover, as long as you use it effectively. Although not as bulky as the engine, the rear bodywork, differential, and tires will give some protection.

A car door won't stop much, even with the glass rolled down. If the bullet strikes the window mechanism, it may be deflected or stopped, but don't bet your life on it.

If you have to use a car door, help the odds by angling it to the direction of the bullets. The sharper the angle, the better, as bullets tend to skid off even auto bodywork at steep angles.

This is much better than using a car door. The entire length of a car body will stop almost anything an opponent can throw at you.

This shows an important point. Unless you're cramped for space, don't snuggle up to your cover, as this one is doing. Keep well back, because you will have more room to move.

This is how to do it. Keeping back from your cover allows you to pop out for a quick shot, then withdraw behind cover quickly, before your adversary can sight in on you. This is much better than this:

Resting the weapon on the car hood takes much longer than swinging your body up for a quick peek and shot. You waste valuable split-seconds that you can't afford.

Popping up over your cover for an instant allows you to get a shot off, without getting involved with securing a rest for your weapon. Protecting yourself is important, so that you can get another shot off.

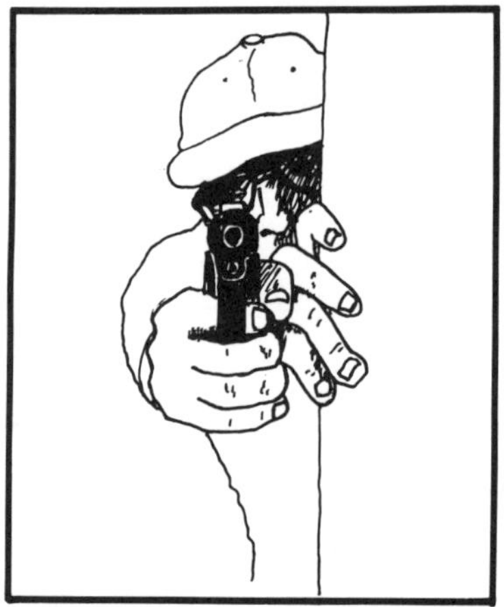

This is another bad tactic, adapted from the obsolete police "barricade" position. Using the corner of the wall to support your weapon is both slow and stupid. You waste time and expose yourself unnecessarily.

Cover can be almost anything, and you can find it almost anywhere.

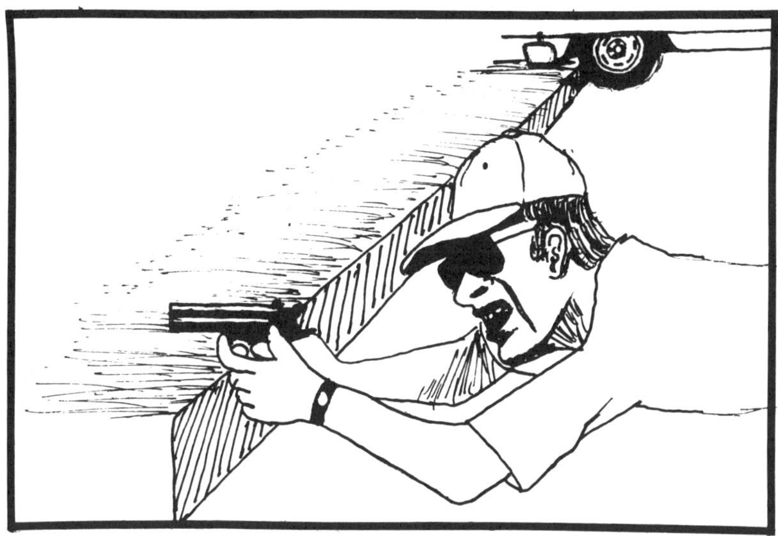

A curb can provide at least partial cover. If nothing else is available, this will have to do.

Outside, we find cover in many places, such as this one that's not too obvious:

From the side, this doesn't look like cover at all. However, the slope provides dead ground, a shallow area hidden from view.

This is what an enemy sees. Most of the body is hidden, and it's quick and easy to roll away into total invisibility.

The tactical use of cover is even more important than the cover itself. Try to pop out from a different point each time, and keep your exposure minimal. Don't let your opponent anticipate where or when you'll be popping out for another shot.

Cover also gives you time to think. Cover provides time to aim carefully, to hit your target and to avoid hitting the wrong person. Cover gives you time to reload in safety. Cover also gives you time to plan tactics.

Remember the space-time cushion. Although a bullet can get to you before you can think about it, with cover you get protection from gunfire. An opponent has to cross the space between himself and you if he wants to get at you.

CONCEALMENT

Concealment is not cover. It's merely protection from view. It's easy to confuse the two, especially if you're a hunter, because hunters use the term cover as a synonym for concealment.

Anything opaque can provide concealment. Sometimes, you find concealment in plain sight, if you take advantage of shadows. Ever notice how the state troopers park their cars under freeway overpasses? Any motorist approaching should be able to see them, because they're in plain sight, but the shadows help conceal them.

Using shrubbery for concealment is okay, as long as you understand clearly that it won't stop a bullet. Two problems with this position are that the shooter is too exposed and is dressed in shades that stand out from the background.

This is better, because of less exposure. Shooting from around and below a bush also places the shooter in the shadow, an important point to remember.

Wearing clothing that blends in helps reduce visibility, even when you expose more body area than necessary.

Shrubbery can make for good concealment, as long as you use it correctly and don't mistake it for cover. Don't listen to those stories about bushes and twigs deflecting the light .223 rifle bullets, either. The people who tell those stories don't stand behind bushes while someone's firing to prove it.

This heroic pose looks great on TV, but what sort of wall is that? Will it stop gunfire from anyone behind that door?

Kicking in doors is TV cop tactics. This flimsy door won't resist a good kick, and it won't stop a bullet.

A better way. Make as small a target of yourself as possible, and ease the door open. Playing commando can get you killed.

FIELDS OF FIRE

This refers to the areas which you can cover with gunfire. It can be very important, because an opponent can protect himself from your bullets even without cover, if he stays out of your field of fire. Let's see how this works:

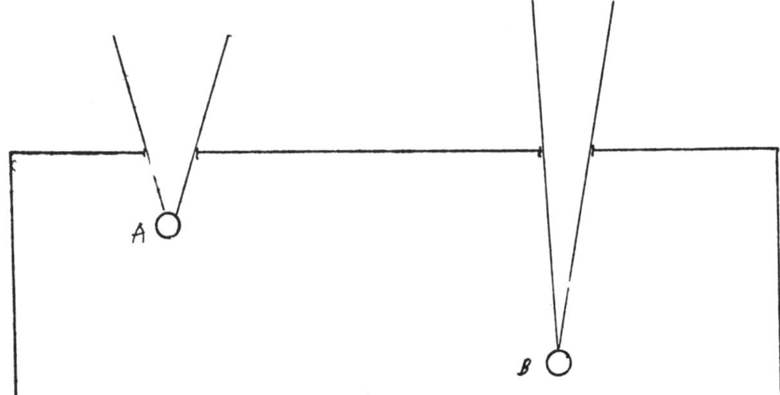

You can see from this diagram that when you're shooting through a doorway or window you have a larger field of fire if

you stand close to it, "A," than if you're back inside the room, at "B." You might choose to stay well inside a room to take advantage of the shadows, reducing your visibility. You also might have found good cover deep inside the room. If you stay deep inside, you'll have to move around to cover different areas outside.

CROSS-FIRE

This means catching an opponent from two different directions. This divides his attention. Gunfire from two directions denies much of the protection of cover, as cross-fire enables shooting around it.

SURPRISE

The value of surprise is obvious, as an adversary caught by surprise is half-disarmed. Using surprise successfully means choosing the moment when the adversary isn't near cover and when he isn't expecting any opposition. He's got to improvise his response under the worst possible conditions, and indeed may be out of the fight before he can decide what to do.

Note that surprise is both an offensive tactic and a defensive one. An ambush of any sort is offensive. Pretending to obey an armed robber, then turning on him, is defensive.

LIGHT

Common sense tells us that keeping to a dark area while the opponent is in a brightly-lit one provides a tactical advantage. What's equally obvious is that the light must not come from you. This is why the "flashlight shooting positions," devised by people who named them after themselves, are really flashlight suicide stances. A flashlight draws fire.

This can be especially evident when dealing with more than one opponent. Even if you can see one of them in the shadowy light, if you decide to dazzle him by shining your light in his eyes, his partner will open fire at the light.

To make the most of light, it must be ambient light. As you know from home defense, having a few night lights on to illuminate an intruder while you remain in darkened rooms gives you most of the advantages.

When you open fire at night, remember that your muzzle flash is visible. Roll away after a couple of shots to avoid the danger from the attacker firing at your flashes.

NUMBERS

It's a basic maxim of military history that, other things being equal, the side with superior numbers will win.[1] This is also true in civilian shoot-outs. Having a partner in a shoot-out doesn't only double your combat power; it squares it.[2] This is because you not only have another gun and pair of eyes on your side, but because you have the ability to act as a team, out-maneuvering a single opponent.

When facing an opponent, you and your partner should spread out. This divides his attention and allows you to catch him in a cross-fire and deny him effective cover.

Team tactics also include pinning an opponent down with gunfire while the other partner rushes or flanks him. It also means that the team members can pace their fire so that they're not all caught reloading at the same moment. A single combatant can't do this, even with a quick reload with an auto pistol.

It's important to understand that numerical strength makes a difference only if other things are approximately equal. Getting several inept people together makes an armed mob, not a coordinated fighting force. Making best use of superior numbers requires skill, training, and coordination. If you're planning armed defense in conjunction with a partner or with several friends, set some time aside for rehearsals. Learn to work together and to anticipate each other's actions.

Work out a basic plan for facing multiple opponents. The simplest way to do this is for each partner to engage the targets on his side, and work his way towards the center. Also learn how to use terrain to get the advantage over superior numbers. Avoid bunching up, because this reduces your baseline and gives an opponent concentrated targets. The worst use of superior numbers is to charge down a corridor together.

RELOADING

With skill and luck, you ought to be able to put your opponent down with a few shots, before your weapon runs empty. If there's more than one opponent, or you're being chased, you can run dry.

Running out of ammunition can be dangerous in certain situations. It's preferable not to be caught with an empty gun. You can easily run out, though. How many people can count their shots accurately while fighting for their lives?

Experienced gunfighters know that the fastest reload is to have a second gun. This is why old Western gunfighters carried two revolvers. They weren't ambidextrous. They just kept that second gun as a reserve. You might consider this. Most likely, though, you'll be armed with only one gun, so let's work on that.

There are two type of reloads used in gunfighting. One is the "normal" reload, when you run out and have to put more ammunition in your weapon to continue firing. The other is the "tactical" reload, when you refill your weapon although you're not yet empty. You are forced to reload when empty, but you may also choose to reload before you run dry. If there's a loaded pause in the action, you may figure that this provides a convenient moment to start off with a fresh load.

Two points about reloading stand out:

1. Always reload behind cover. Even if you're taking a tactical reload, and you have one in the chamber, you're out of action for a moment and you don't want to be caught in the open with an inoperative weapon.
2. Reload before changing position. You might need to fire while on the move or upon reaching cover, and you're better off with a full gun. Only if you have to, fire while in the open, should you ever get caught short, but even then, it's better to run for cover than to stand still and reload.

DON'T BE RUSHED

Although your life may be on the line, in many situations you've got time to spare. This is especially true in defensive positions, where you can keep behind cover and ambush an attacker. Taking your time means that you're more likely to make the correct decisions, and avoid some obvious errors such as firing at the wrong person.

PRACTICE TACTICS

Keeping your proficiency with a weapon requires some live fire. Practicing tactics doesn't. You can practice with dart guns, water pistols, and even empty-handed. Whatever you do, practice your tactics with the same devotion you give to your gun-handling skill. Use mental rehearsals to keep yourself sharp, and to practice adapting to different situations. Keep your tactics sharp and you'll come out better if ever you go to war.

NOTES

1. *Understanding War,* Trevor N. Dupuy, New York, Paragon House, 1987, p. 6.
2. *Ibid.,* pp. 18-20.

YOUR HOME IS YOUR CASTLE — MAYBE

The place you choose to live determines much of your vulnerability to crime. It's easy to say that you should live in a nice neighborhood, supposedly free of drug traffic and other hazards, but moving there can be a serious financial problem. Also keep in mind that nice neighborhoods are precisely the ones which burglars and intruders are hitting harder and more often these days. The way a burglar sees it, if you live in a nice area you have more property worth stealing.

Choosing a place to live is only the first step. Making it defensible is the rest of it. Let's look at the various features of a home that can improve or worsen your prospects of defending it. We'll also discuss alarms and locks briefly, examining how they fit into an overall defense plan.

Once you've decided on the neighborhood, you have to choose between a house or an apartment. A house is a better choice for several reasons. Apartments have their advantages, too, and let's take a look at them before we proceed:

1. They're usually smaller which means there's less space you need to defend.
2. There's usually only one door, more solid than those usually found in private houses.
3. Apartments above ground level make it harder for an intruder to climb into your windows.

The disadvantages of living in an apartment are:

1. People. Many inhabitants are transients. Neighbors don't know each other, and don't look out for each other. Privacy seems to be the most important value; "Mind your own business and I'll mind mine." Your neighbor's not going to be concerned about strange people or noises that don't intrude into his own living space.
2. Some older apartments have fire escapes, making easy routes for intruders. This forces you to deny access through your windows, too. Windows are hard to defend, as a lock doesn't stop a burglar. A good defense is an iron grill, but this usually requires the landlord's permission.
3. It's harder to survey your home upon arrival, as your windows may be high off the ground. This makes it harder to see if the lights and the curtains are still the way you left them.

AN APARTMENT CHECKLIST

- Pick an apartment above ground level to make it harder for a burglar. If it has to be on the ground floor, install grills. That can make it feel like living in prison, though.

- Some apartments have flimsy doors. If yours is one of the old ones with a frosted glass panel, replace the door or find somewhere else to live.
- Make sure that it's easy to see the windows from the street. It's important to give them a once-over when you come home.
- Look over the hallways, stairs, and elevators carefully for dark corners. Are there any spots that offer good ambush points for a mugger? Is your front door hidden in an alcove, or can you see it when you get out of the elevator?

LIVING IN A HOUSE

A house offers a number of advantages:

1. There's more defensible space around a house. You may spot the intruders crossing the yard.
2. There's actually more real privacy, because there aren't any people walking up and down your hallway. You can challenge anyone crossing your lawn. You'll also find few strangers coming right up to your windows.
3. Neighbors are friendlier, and more concerned and aware of the state of the neighborhood. A *Blockwatch* operation's got a better chance.

Some disadvantages are:

1. Many houses are more isolated than apartments, with no common wall with other dwellings. A lot could happen in your house with nobody else aware of it.
2. The doors and windows are often very insecure. Most are at ground level, very accessible to in-

truders. Some features, such as arcadia doors, are extremely vulnerable.

3. Many have rear entrances hidden from outside view. This makes breaking and entering easy. Fences aggravate the problem. An intruder could park a pick-up truck in your carport and make off with your property without being seen by neighbors.

MAKING A HOUSE SECURE

The precautions to take are more extensive than with an apartment because the possibilities are greater:

1. Select a house that doesn't have many of the obvious weaknesses such as arcadia doors, and front and kitchen doors with windows. Some have windows close enough to the door to enable a burglar to reach in to unlock the door after cutting through the glass. This is almost hopeless, because most houses have one or more of these.
2. Choose a house with few windows. Windows too small to allow an adult to pass are more desirable. These save energy and make it hard on an intruder.
3. There should be at least one window on each side of your house to avoid blind spots.
4. Shrubbery shouldn't be too heavy to prevent inspecting your doors and windows from the street. This allows checking out the house before entering.

5. Brick or block construction provide the best protection from gunfire. Shots fired inside should not exit to threaten neighbors.
6. Any back door should be visible from the side or the alley. An excessively high fence can be a problem.
7. Large trees on your property can serve as cover for an assailant.

Buying a house offers you more possibilities for defense because you have more latitude for installing defensive features without anyone's permission or even knowledge. This is important, because defensive measures that are very conspicuous and elaborate advertise that there's something especially worth protecting inside.

Alarms

Passive defenses have their place because the risk from burglary is much greater than the risk from robbery. It would be ironic to find your stock of weapons stolen by a burglar after leaving your home unattended all day. We'll give some of these a once-over.

Commercial alarm systems can be quite sophisticated and very costly. A price of one thousand dollars for a system to cover a small house is not out of line. There are several possibilities. You can have it react to intrusion only or you may include fire sensors. The control box can ring an alarm on the premises or send a taped message to the police. Another type involves a security company, which receives the alarm signal and sends its own security agents to check it out. This service costs at least thirty dollars per month.

If price is no object, all sorts of sensors are available. These will detect an intruder who manages to bypass the perimeter sensors. Infra-red sensors detect body heat, and ultra-sonic sensors detect motion. Pets, however, can set off some of these sensors inadvertently.

Do-it-yourself alarms are cost-effective. In some cases, they're deterrents, because the sensors and wires are visible from outside. Some alarm kits include stickers to warn off intruders.

The main value of an alarm system is protecting your life by warning of an entry when you're home. Whatever system you install, make sure that it wakes you first. One that rings a gong on the outside of your house isn't much help if it's not loud enough to awaken you. An external gong can alert neighbors when you're away, though.

The cost of a do-it-yourself system starts at about one hundred dollars. They can include sophisticated sensors, including infra-red, ultrasound, and seismic detectors. Seismic detectors have their problems, though. Although one attached to a wall can detect the breaking of a window, any blow against that wall will set it off.

The most cost-effective alarms are the cheapest, because they're simple and quick to install, and you can take them with you to make an office or hotel room secure. A capacitance alarm costs between twenty and thirty dollars. This hangs on a doorknob, and reacts if anyone touches that knob. For under ten dollars, an alarm with a blade switch is available to protect a door or window. The blade goes into the crack of the door or window. Opening releases the pressure on the blade, closing the contact.

If you're lucky enough to live in an area with many like-minded neighbors, you can rig a system of alarms to ring in each other's homes. This allows neighbors to be alerted when intrusions occur, so that they may take appropriate action.

If you're interested in setting up alarms, books on the subject are commonly available. The Yellow Pages list alarm dealers, and you'll find that the instructions packed with the hardware are often all you need to know.

Locks, And Other Defenses

Special doors to resist forced entry are expensive. So is grillwork. Rolling shutter doors cost hundreds of dollars. Steel doors to replace wooden outer doors cost about three hundred dollars each, complete with steel frame. A steel door without the steel frame offers far less protection.

In some high-crime areas, people put steel bars across their doors to prevent break-ins. A lesser measure, if you have an arcadia door, is to put a bar in the bottom track to keep the door shut in case anyone slips the cheap lock.

Locks won't stop the "pro," but will deter the amateur. The real function of a lock on a door or window is not to absolutely shut out intruders when you're not there, but to keep them from surprising you when you are. The noise of a breaking door or window should awaken you from a sound sleep. Be sure, however, that you use dead-bolt locks on your doors, not the spring-loaded ones that can be *slipped* with a credit card.

There's a limit to these modifications. High-visibility measures that protect a business are acceptable, but you may not want your house looking like a fortress. If you don't object, your wife will.

Lighting For Defense

Many criminals come out at night, feeling that the darkness gives them an edge. On your territory, you can manipulate the lighting to your best advantage. A system of outside lights makes a trespasser visible long before he reaches your house. You can see who's coming, and how many there are, but they can't see you. Outside lighting also silhouettes anyone coming in through a door or window.

Outside lights can make it very uncomfortable for anyone trying to break in. Install several for all-around protection.

Place your outside lights so that they don't shine right in your windows. You want to keep the inside dark.

If you have had problems with trespassers, installing a system of floodlights controlled from inside can help you to identify them as you startle them with glaring lights. One point to watch is the location of the switches. Outside light switches are usually next to a door but they don't have to be. Place them where you have the best advantage.

In many instances, it's a good idea to keep a light on in a room that you're defending. Under no circumstances should you be in a room with the lights on, but rather in another room where you can see into the illuminated one. The room you're defending will usually be the first one an intruder enters, such as the living room, or an outer office in your work-place. It's normal to leave a night light on, and the intruder won't be expecting an ambush.

Night lights can illuminate an intruder while you wait in the shadows to ambush him.

In certain situations the lights may be out. You'd want them out if you've placed obstructions in the intruder's path. You might want the lights out in case of a riot, to avoid revealing occupancy. If you leave all of the lights out, you'll need to be very alert.

Usually, emergency lighting, except for a flashlight and some *Cyalume* Light-sticks, isn't worth it. Generator-powered emergency lights would be psychologically reassuring but tactically not very useful.

As we've seen, using a flashlight to locate or to dazzle an intruder is a very bad idea. There are better ways.

One way is to turn on the lights from the next room. If you have your weapon ready, you'll have the suspect covered before he realizes what's happened.

Another way to light up a suspect is with a Cyalume Light-stick. The technique for pitching it into the next room without giving him warning or illuminating yourself is as follows:

Tear one end off the envelope holding the Light-stick. Keeping the Light-stick in its envelope, bend it sharply to break the capsule and activate the light. Still holding it in its envelope, swing it and let the Light-stick slip out of the envelope as you throw it.

If the room's already lit with a night light, but the intruder's behind cover, throwing something to land behind him will cause a sudden noise from a direction he doesn't expect.

The Safe Room

Another idea for home security is that of a "safe room." This room has a strong door, reinforced walls, a telephone and a radio. In case of intrusion this room will be a refuge for you and your family. You lock the intruders out and call for help on the telephone or the radio, and if the police are not having too busy a night they'll show up.

A safe room can be a trap. Retreating to a safe room is a bad tactic. It limits your freedom of action because at the outset you relinquish the rest of your house or apartment to the intruder. While you're locked in, and the police are on the way, the intruders can loot your home bare.

While a telephone in the bathroom is sometimes a good idea because the phone always seems to ring at the wrong moment, using the bathroom as a safe room has its limitations. The only advantage the bathroom has is that some of its fixtures offer some protection against gunfire. Otherwise, there is the same problem. You're not defending your living space.

The Defensive Core

This can be a room, but it isn't necessary. It's a central place from which you can defend your home, and it can be an alcove or hallway. All it needs is fields of fire and protection from an assailant's gunfire.

The core should be in a place that no intruder can enter directly from outside. You don't want to lose the tactical advantage by having an intruder in the same room with you. It's very uncomfortable to share a room with an armed intruder. It's even worse to be in a room with an opening to the outside in case of a public disturbance.

Making the most of a defensive position requires a little restructuring of the house and rearranging of the furniture. You need to establish a good defensive position without giving your home the appearance of a fortress.

Choose a place that gives you a good view of the rest of your home. The drawing below shows one arrangement:

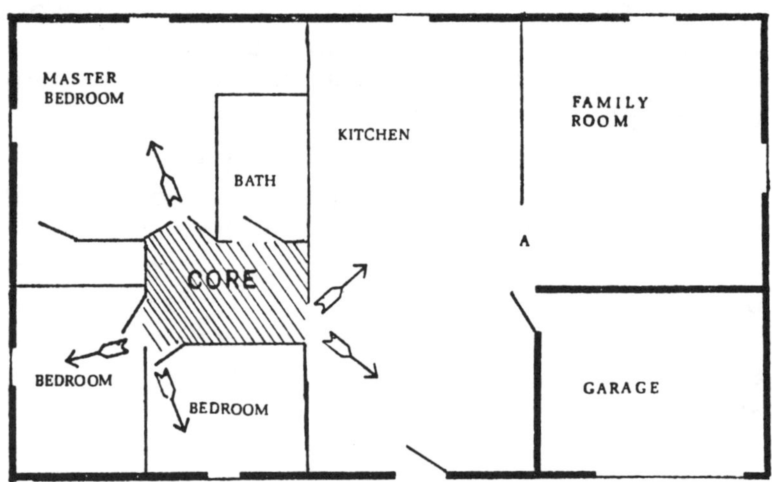

This set-up provides several good fields of fire as well as several escape routes, if they should become necessary. What's not as obvious is protection from gunfire.

In a house with very stout walls, such as stone or adobe, cover already exists. Few people are so fortunate. There are ways to fortify a house without making it obvious. One is filling the hollow interior walls with sand up to a height of about three feet. This doesn't leave any conspicuous traces. Drilling a hole several feet up the wall, pouring in the sand, and re-plastering and painting, will accomplish this task in a very inconspicuous way. Sand stops bullets well, depending on the type of sand. To get an idea of what the sand available in your area will do, take a coffee can full with you next time you go shooting. Fire a bullet into it to check penetration. You'll be surprised at how well it stops bullets.

Another way is using hidden steel plates. It's not too difficult to obtain steel plates ¼" thick to fit inside closets and bathroom cabinets to protect you from gunfire. A couple of bolts will hold them in place, out of sight. If no closets are in convenient locations, wood paneling will cover the steel plates so as not to reveal the armoring to a casual observer.

If you need to provide bullet-resistant windows, replacing the glass with ⅜" thick polycarbonate will provide a pane that will stop pistol bullets up to a .38 Special. Polycarbonate is sold under the names of *Lexan* and *Tuffak*. You can send for a leaflet on its use from:

Rohm and Haas
Marketing Services
Independence Mall West
Philadelphia, PA 19105

This leaflet has photos and drawings that clearly show how to use polycarbonate to reinforce windows and doors.

DEFENDING THE CORE

The crucial point about a defensive core is using it in a tactically sound way. As a start, you need warning of an intrusion, and we'll examine in detail how to arrange this.

The worst thing that can happen to you is to wake up with the intruder in the room with you. You'll have no time to draw and fire before he's on top of you.

The location provides fields of fire in several directions so that the defender can dominate the approaches to the bedrooms and the bathroom. This allows his family some protection.

Interior walls are flimsy, and the defender can fire through them in case an intruder uses one of them for concealment.

Part of the plan is minimizing any cover and concealment available to an intruder. This means placing only lightly-built furniture in the areas immediately accessible to the intruder. It's not enough to plan the inside of the house this way. The yard must not provide cover or concealment for a trespasser. It's a good idea to remove large trees and to keep bushes small.

Fences offer some privacy and the illusion of protection, but unless you can see through them they provide concealment to anyone approaching. A low fence or a wire fence isn't as objectionable because it allows you to see beyond it. If you must have a fence, build a wooden slat fence. This won't afford cover to anyone approaching.

Let's look at specific features of a home and assess their defensive potential:

Windows

You should inspect every window in your home and consider three points:

1. Can an intruder get in because it's low enough to the ground, or has a fire escape?

2. Is there anything I can do to make access harder?
3. Can an attacker throw something in?

Some windows, such as those in bathrooms, are too small to afford access. Others, such as those in a garage, allow entry only to a remote area, where the intruder can't threaten you or your family directly. You'll want to defend these against burglars, but a forced intrusion isn't a high priority.

There are two ways you can protect your windows, blocking and warning. Blocking means denying access. Warning is to make it impossible for anyone to enter without making noise or otherwise alerting you.

A bare window can be very vulnerable if at ground level. Don't leave it bare. Put knick-knacks on the window sill. Glass or ceramic objects that shatter make excellent alarms. Double-insure by placing objects on the floor to trip anyone coming through a window.

You can block your window by putting a hefty lock on it, but the strongest lock doesn't help when it's merely holding shut a large pane of glass. A grill provides much more protection; and is more expensive. If you decide on a grill, be sure that it's not mounted with bolts that are removable from the outside.

A sheet of polycarbonate plastic inside each pane of glass is much less conspicuous, and provides protection against thrown objects.

The advantage of protecting windows this way is that a trespasser can't simply break the glass by using wet newspaper or masking tape to muffle the noise, reach in and open the lock. The noise of breaking through polycarbonate will give plenty of warning if you're home.

Another way of providing warning is by small alarms on each window. These can be the battery-powered spring clip type. The main advantages of these are that they're inexpensive and can't be deactivated by cutting the power to the house.

Doors And Doorways

Doors are usually more secure than windows because they're more heavily built. The same sorts of grills and alarms can protect doorways. The main purposes are to discourage entry when you're not home, and to prevent anyone from coming in on you unexpectedly when you are.

If someone gets into your home and starts working his way towards you, you ought to be prepared to defend a doorway. This is very much like defending a room, and the same principle applies. Never defend a room from the inside if possible. Try to defend it from the next room.

There are several ways of penetrating or assaulting a doorway: slipping or flitting in, jumping or diving in, and the roll-and-fire commando type entry. There are only two defenses: obstructions and firepower.

Obstructions and alarms can defeat a stealthy entry. Arrange furniture so that an intruder tripping over it can alert you and cause him an injury. If you have warning of a stealthy entry, gunfire while the intruder's silhouetted in the doorway will also stop him.

These methods will also stop the "flit," another type of stealthy entry that minimizes the amount of time spent in the doorway. The intruder may peek around the doorway for an instant, then slip around the jamb to wind up on the same side as he started, but inside the room. This is no protection if you're alert, because a couple of shots on that side of the door jamb will probably hit him.

The more violent entries, such as the diagonal dash, dive, and roll, are likely to be the methods chosen by violent intruders, such as thrill killers. The basic idea of all of these commando style methods is to get in fast before the defender can react.

Obstructions can be extremely effective in breaking up such attacks. Anyone diving in onto chair legs will be hurt. Hard objects, such as roller skates left on the floor, will break a few ribs. Anyone trying the roll-and-fire method will find his aim upset by crashing into hard objects as he rolls in.

The roll-and-fire attack shows up the danger of being in the same room with the attacker. An attacker who throws in a few shots to prepare his way might get lucky and hit you. If he continues to fire on the way in, it can become very unhealthy in the room.

DEFENDING A ROOM

Protecting your home against a dangerous intruder often comes down to defending a particular room. Let's begin by repeating the prime law regarding room defense, one which almost everyone ignores:

Always defend a room from the next one, if possible. The worst place to be is inside the room you're defending. An attacker may dive in on you, you don't want desperate hand-to-hand combat if you've got a weapon. Some intruders are fairly sophisticated, and may spray tear gas from a spray can into the room before entering. A really nasty "biker" type may throw in a bottle of gasoline. Another unpleasant prospect in home defense is that the intruder may dash by you and get between you and your family before you can react and neutralize him.

When defending a room from the next one, you should pick a room with two exits. You don't want to be trapped. Sometimes you have no choice. Whatever the case, leave a light on in the room you're defending, and keep all lights out in the room you're occupying. Leave the door between them open so that nothing keeps you from seeing and hearing anything that happens in that room. You can always slam it shut if the situation calls for it. The next door, through which an attack may come, may be closed or open, depending on your preference. Also try to have a light on in the room beyond, to silhouette an attacker in the doorway.

Sometimes the layout simply won't permit your defending a room from the next one. If you're forced to defend it from inside, always stay behind cover, or at least concealed. Keep the lights out, to protect yourself. This is so important that you ought to take a couple of minutes to ensure that no intruder can light you up by reaching around a corner to a light switch. Unscrew every bulb or pull every lamp cord. If you're pressed for time and noise doesn't matter, break the bulbs. At the same time, a good tactic is to have the lights on in the room from which the attack will come.

Always keep an obstruction between yourself and the doorway. You don't want to give any attacker a clear run at you, even if he knows where you are. If absolutely necessary, you might retreat to a closet. This leaves you trapped, but sometimes you have no choice. Leave the closet door open, though, to give you a clear shot at your attacker.

REACTION

Once the physical preparations are complete, the rest is up to you. Set up a meeting with your family to discuss the plans. Decide whether the best course will be "fight" or "flight." A good compromise is to have your family flee, if an alternate exit is available, while you cover the retreat. It's best to rehearse several plans with your family, both to check if they're practical and to make sure they know what to do.

If you're awakened by a noise, you have to move quickly, yet avoid an impulsive reaction. Your weapon should be loaded and ready to go, but you should not open fire on a family member returning from the kitchen. This is why the initial step should be to check on the members of your family to make sure that they're where you expect them to be. If the intrusion is real, you'll need to have your family in a safe area or leaving the scene. Telephoning the police isn't necessarily the first priority, as your family can do this after they leave. Once the first problems are out of the way, the next step is a reconnaissance to find out how many intruders there are and where they are.

Giving your home a once-over does not mean getting a flashlight and walking around examining the doors and windows. A flashlight can get you killed. The first reconnaissance is by sound. Sit still and listen. You may hear unusual noises, the sounds of movement, or of a window being eased open. Make use of the night lights you've left on. Stick to the shadows and let the suspects show themselves when they move. Remember that you're not in a hurry. You know your territory and the intruder doesn't. Make use of this advantage.

Another reason for going slowly is that you don't have to be in a hurry to leave your defensive core. Never let any intruder get between you and your family. This is not only to protect them, but because any shots you fire should be away from your family.

Once you locate the intruder or intruders, decide how you're going to cope with the situation. You may decide to simply ambush them when they get within your defensive perimeter. This is usually the safest course, because going after them may put you in a tactically bad spot. However, if you've planned thoroughly, you'll have several advance defensive positions earmarked, and you can choose one to fit the situation.

It's normal to feel fear. Don't let it break you up. If you've planned and rehearsed properly, you'll have helped to cope with the fear reaction. You might, however, find that your hands are shaking so much you can barely aim your weapon. This is why your plans should include resting the weapon on a piece of furniture if you have to.

A major mistake would be to pursue the intruders outside your home. One reason is that once the threat to life ceases, you no longer have a legal right to deadly force, and the other concerns the reaction of the police if they see you with a gun outside.

DAYLIGHT INTRUSIONS

In most parts of the country, intruders don't attempt attacks when the occupants are inside and awake. In states without repressive gun control laws, breaking in could get them shot for their trouble. There are, however, a few bold or crazy ones who will try it. Some prowl neighborhoods looking for open windows or unlocked doors. In some instances, they ring the bell and assault whoever answers.

The basic precaution is to keep both doors and windows locked to prevent anyone entering without your knowledge. Along with this, you should never open the door unless you know who is on the other side. A peephole in the door is one way to do this, but the tiny optical peepholes are almost useless. A decorative cover backed up by a piece of Lexan gives you a much better view. A window near the door is even better because you can check someone out without being seen. If you feel truly endangered, make it standard practice never to open the door for anyone you don't know. This is good general practice, even in areas with low violent crime rates, because it prevents many possible problems.

Anyone can claim to be a telephone repairman or "gas main inspector." Credentials are easy to forge, and unless you have previously seen genuine ones, even a crude forgery can fool you. There are confidence tricksters who pose as repairmen and inspectors to sell you shoddy repairs and alterations. If you haven't sent for a telephone serviceman, don't admit anyone who claims to be one. He might be a con-man, or he might be a rapist.

Another precaution is to ask your friends to phone you before they visit. This is normal courtesy in many areas, but it's also an important security measure. Don't let this lull your alertness, because a robber might, just by coincidence, ring your bell about the time you're expecting company.

If you live in a high-risk area, carrying a weapon with you at all times can be a sensible precaution. Intruders have been known to crash in through windows. A pistol in your pocket or on your belt will be with you at all times, without conscious effort from you. If you don't have a pistol, a shoulder weapon will do it, but only if you keep it within reach at all times. Keeping the weapon with you always is the key point. Take it into the bathroom with you. If you have to leave it behind you, as when you take a shower, lock the bathroom door. Another precaution is to keep window curtains and blinds always drawn enough to prevent anyone from peering in to observe you.

Answering the door is the critical point. The wrong ways to do it are to open the door without first looking and asking, and to remain within reach of anyone coming in. The better way is to unlock the door quietly after you're satisfied regarding the identity of the caller. Back off across the room before calling for him to come in. If you feel that the caller is truly doubtful, you can keep a weapon in your hand but hidden by a doorway as you watch him come in.

You might ask at this point; "Why open the door at all? Isn't it better to refuse admittance to anyone I don't know?" There are exceptions to every rule. If you normally have your groceries delivered, the grocery boy doesn't normally carry ID. You might be expecting groceries, but not recognize the face because the regular grocery boy has been replaced or is ill. You might be expecting the exterminator, and they usually don't carry credentials, either. Keeping a weapon close at hand is your insurance policy.

COMING HOME TO AN INTRUDER

One of the worst things you can do is to walk in on an intruder. Despite the truism that burglars aren't armed because they prefer to work by stealth, enough intruders are armed and dangerous to make it very risky for you to blunder in unawares. The intruder may panic, especially if you're standing between him and the only exit. In an extreme case, he may take you and your wife hostage while he prepares for the Siege of Alcatraz.

This is why you should never let yourself into your home, or let any other family member in, until you've checked the place out for signs of forced entry. Drive or walk around the block. Is there a strange vehicle parked in front of your house? Is the engine running? Take a look down the alley. Look for anything out of place, and look for suspicious signs such as a ladder or trash barrel up against your back wall. Check for details such as these:

1. Doors or windows open.
2. Curtains or venetian blinds disturbed.
3. Lights that were not on when you left.
4. Check the knick-knacks on the windows sills. Are they still there?

5. Is there a car or truck parked in your driveway or carport?

If you live in an apartment, you'll be happy to be able to see your front door as soon as you get out of the elevator, instead of having it hidden in an alcove. If you own a house, checking it out shows you the value of keeping shrubbery cleared from the doors and windows.

If you find signs of intrusion, there are several things to do and not to do. First, don't play "macho man" and go in after a possible intruder. This is what's gotten several people killed recently. Staying away is also good advice to follow if you see your neighbor's home being burglarized. If you enter, you're the one advancing into territory controlled by the intruder, and this places you at a terrible tactical disadvantage.

A good first step is to call the police. It's really their job to handle situations such as this, and they can arrive with enough manpower to make resistance very risky for any criminal.

One problem this brings is that the police may not respond quickly enough. You'd be very put out having to watch a burglar carry off your possessions, and tempted to act. Remember that you can open fire only to save your life, not your property. If you shoot at anyone driving away with your stereo, you're in trouble. This doesn't mean that you can't stop a thief by other means.

One way of disabling his vehicle is to take his ignition key, if it's still in place for a quick get-away. Another is to park your vehicle to block his. Slashing his tires isn't a really good solution, because in a pinch it's possible to drive a vehicle with four flats. If it's a stolen vehicle, and the intruder doesn't care about additional damage, he may do just that. Opening his hood and ripping out his ignition wires is a much surer method. If the hood's locked, reaching under the vehicle and slashing his gas line and coolant hoses will cause him problems.

More desperate ways are to shoot into the engine compartment or set fire to the vehicle. It's not necessary to set fire to the whole vehicle. Pouring some charcoal lighter fluid onto the driver's seat and lighting it will definitely prevent him from driving away. Any other inflammable substance, even wadded newspapers, will do if you place it in the driver's seat. The problem with setting a fire is that, even though you're doing it for a good cause, you may set yourself up for a charge of arson.

Tactically, if your method of disabling his vehicle is noisy, you'll throw away the advantage of surprise. You may prefer to take cover outside your house and wait for the intruder to leave.

CLEARING A HOUSE

Another possibility is that you've seen signs of entry but nothing to indicate that the intruder's still inside. Don't be in a hurry to enter and assess the damage. If the intruder's still inside, he may ambush you. If you've got the choice, you may prefer to wait for the police and let them "clear" the house.

If you live in an isolated location, and have to do it yourself, there are certain points to watch. Look the premises over thoroughly before approaching. If you think that anyone inside hasn't detected your approach, wait to see if there are any signs of life inside. If you see nothing to show that the premises are occupied, make your way closer, using cover and concealment. Get next to the outside wall and listen for sounds from inside.

Don't open any doors or windows yet. Instead, approach any that were left open. Peek quickly inside. Be sure to scrutinize the area you can see through the crack on the hinge side of the door. You want to guard against the chance that a burglar's waiting for you behind the door.

The wrong way to do it, even with help. Anyone behind the door can pump a few bullets through it. Standing right in the doorway after opening the door is a suicidal tactic.

If the door's not open, push it open, keeping to the side, and wait for at least a minute for a reaction. Don't rush: you've got all the time in the world. Just as importantly, don't try any commando tactics such as diving in, rolling, and firing. You're only an army of one, and can't afford any casualties.

As a preliminary step, take a quick peek from behind the doorway. Don't linger, but pull your head back immediately to avoid giving anyone inside a target. If you see anyone, don't study him or her, but pull back immediately. Take another quick peek from lower down a few seconds later. This cuts the risk of someone sighting in on the doorway and snapping a shot off at you when you reappear.

If everything's clear, creep in, making sure that you stay well clear of any concealment an intruder might use to ambush you. Don't lead with your weapon because an opponent might grab it while you're negotiating a corner, especially if you creep along the wall. Go wide around a corner, and keep your eyes and ears open. Staying well back from the corner, gradually move to the side, so that you can see more of the area behind the corner as you move. Keep the area covered with your weapon, prepared to fire if you see any hostile person.

Before moving from one room to the next, check out everything in that room. Look behind and under furniture where a person might hide. Don't turn your back on any doors you haven't checked out first. Open every closet to make sure that nobody's using it as a hiding place. Look behind every curtain. Look under desks, tables, and inside cabinets. Check the space under every sink. In the bathroom, check the shower enclosure. Always remember not to lead with your weapon, because this exposes it to snatching.

Do you close and lock doors after passing through them? That depends on whether your purpose is to clear the house and give anyone inside the chance of making a break for it, or whether you want to trap him and hold him for the police. As a practical point, it's hard to trap an intruder if you're alone, because exits are so vulnerable. Even with double dead-bolts on the doors, he can open a window and dive out, unless you live in an apartment several floors up.

PETS

A dog will often bark when a stranger approaches. Because his senses are far more acute than yours, he's a biological early-warning system. Some cats, also, will alert you to the approach of a stranger to the home. They don't make noise, however, and you'll become aware of this only if you're awake and looking at them when they *freeze* and look in the direction of the noise.

Early warning is the only purpose a pet should serve for your home defense. Some people contemplate getting guard or attack dogs, but there are a couple of problems with these. One is cost. A properly trained attack dog is costly, and can run you several thousands of dollars. Another is liability. A dog who attacks someone without justification can land you in very hot water. As the owner, you're legally liable, and the court won't show you any sympathy.

WHEN THE POLICE ARRIVE

The odds are that sooner or later the police will arrive, probably after it's all over. There are several ways this can come about, however, and it's important that you understand the likely course of events in each case.

One way is that a police patrol may notice a window open in your home, or a car parked outside when normally the street is clear. Any such clue can cause the police to stop and investigate.

Another way is that a neighbor called them, having either seen suspicious activity or heard shots. Either way, the police will come looking for suspects, and they probably won't know who you are if they see you. This is why you should not be walking around with a weapon. The cops can easily mistake you for a suspect, especially in dim light.

The third case is if you or a family member call the police. It's important to stay on the line, if possible, and to describe the situation to the police dispatcher completely. If your wife calls the police, she should describe you, and tell them whether the suspect is still on the premises. Do this before letting the police in. This is critically important if you've captured the suspect and are holding him at gun point.

EXTRA EQUIPMENT

A fire extinguisher can be very helpful in case of an intrusion. A gas mask can pay its way, especially now that there are available some very good surplus Israeli civilian gas masks for ten or twenty dollars.

ARMED DEFENSE IN THE WORKPLACE

If you're employed in certain fields, you're much more likely to face an armed aggressor at work than at home. Some of the top targets for robbers are convenience store clerks, gas station employees, and taxi drivers. Patterns of victimization vary with the area of the country and even with the year. In certain areas of the Southwest, convenience stores are held up so often that they're sometimes called "Stop 'n Robs."

Robbers prefer to strike when the employee is alone, for tactical reasons, as we'll soon see. This suggests that the graveyard shift is more dangerous than the day or evening shift.

COMPANY POLICY

Your response to a robber or burglar will depend on whether you're the owner or just an employee. It's ironic that the types of businesses facing the most common risks tend to have employees who have the least at stake in defending property. Banks, gas stations, and convenience markets are frequent targets, yet have reputations of paying their employees poorly. They also tend to treat employees in a casual, offhand way that does not build employee loyalty.

Some corporations have a positive disregard for employees' safety. Convenience stores, in particular, have strict policies that employees are not to carry weapons, and not to resist a robber. Several convenience store clerks have been fired for using weapons against robbers. This is more out of concern over a possible lawsuit if an employee shoots the wrong person, than concern over employee safety. They even refuse to take the simplest measures to protect employees, such as issuing uniforms with ballistic panels.

Employee

If you happen to work in this sort of business you have two choices. The first is whether you should try protecting the boss's property. There's no point in defending what the employer doesn't want defended, especially if rules forbid firearms on the job. If you're earning minimum wage or slightly more you can be sure that your employer thinks of you as a paper towel. When he's through with them he throws them away.

The other choice relates to defending your life. Some robbers don't like to leave witnesses. This places you in great danger. If you can afford it, buy and wear a bullet-resistant vest under your shirt or uniform tunic. You also have to ask yourself if you're willing to carry and use a weapon to defend your life. Company policy, and the threat of getting fired doesn't matter anymore when you're facing the sort of robber who exterminates witnesses.

Owner

If you're the owner, you have a lot at stake. You may have had an alarm system installed. This may be a burglar alarm or a silent alarm aimed against robbers. You may even be paying a security service to patrol your premises after closing time.

Silent alarms have their drawbacks. Response time can be too slow. Police or security guards rarely arrive in time to apprehend the robbers. This puts it up to you. If you have employees willing to help, you're lucky. At the outset, you must understand that your situation is far worse than that of a householder because he doesn't have to cope with a flow of strangers passing through his property all day. You have a steady stream of customers, and one of them might turn out to be a robber.

DEFENSE

There are three phases to protection at work, just as there are at home. You need practical preparations, early warning, and direct action. An additional problem is the presence of innocent people in the area.

Because your clients have a right to be on your premises, you can't take action until the robbery *comes down.* This dictates that any counter-measures be absolutely defensive. A practical basic step is to be wearing a ballistic vest. This is not a step a householder would usually take, but it's worth considering for a businessman in high-risk areas.

Another practical step is to set up advanced firing positions. This means protected positions behind a counter or doorway which will shelter you from gunfire and give you the opportunity of shooting it out with a robber, if that's what you wish. The way to prepare these positions is to insert steel plates into the counters and steel or sand into the walls. When laying out the positions, try to select those which provide fields of fire separated by about 90 degrees. This allows converging fire on a robber, and minimizes the cover he can use.

The next step is planning your customer area to reduce the cover and concealment available to a robber. Arranging displays so that they're below head height is one important step. The next is coordinating displays with your fire plan. You may have some displays which may stop bullets, such as canned food. Place such displays only where all four sides are visible from your protected positions.

The choice of weapons is the final decision. Wearing a concealed handgun is the best way to cope with a robbery. Even the dullest robber can figure out that a shopkeeper might have a weapon concealed in the cash drawer or next to it. This is why any such weapon will probably wind up in the robber's hands. He won't allow you near the cash register, instead choosing to rummage through it himself.

Layout

Let's look at a typical store plan to illustrate some protective steps:

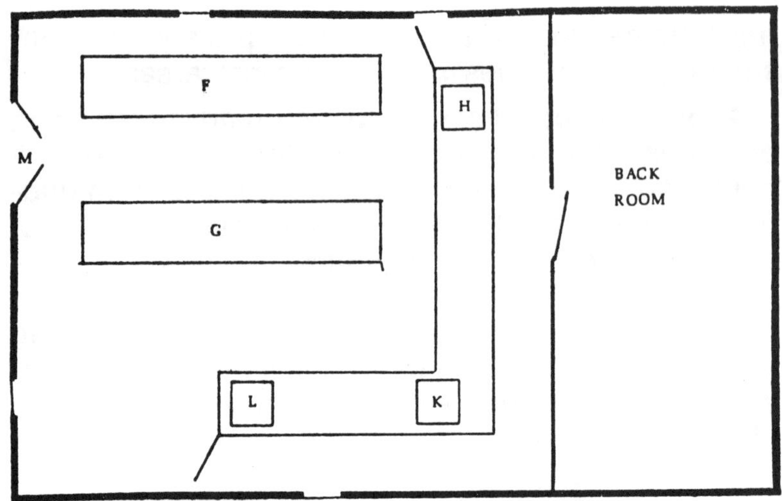

This simplified plan shows what could be a convenience market, drug store, etc. The front area is the important one, and it has three counters. Two are lightly-built and in the customer area. These should never be above chest height and should hold only light goods that won't stop bullets. Anything heavier or more solid, such as cans of motor oil, should be on the L-shaped counter to provide cover for the staff.

On the L-shaped counter, there are cash registers at "L" and "H." There are steel plates inside the counter below the cash registers and the stack of cans. These provide firing positions that almost totally deny the robbers concealment or cover behind the counters because of cross-fire.

Early Warning

You won't get much early warning. Robbers don't make appointments. However, some of them may alert you to their plans by their behavior, if you're not too busy taking care of customers to take notice.

A. A customer who browses or lingers longer than most may just be waiting for the premises to empty before robbing you. Robbers like few people around because additional people bring risks. One might be an off-duty cop, or a civilian who wants to be a hero.

B. A customer who leaves his car engine running, or who has a driver stay in the car while he comes in.

C. Customers who seem to be observing you and other customers more than looking at the merchandise.

D. A suspicious bulge in clothing might signify a hidden weapon.

E. You may notice someone easing around the counter, or to a corner behind you. Another sign is two customers approaching you from both sides at once, bracketing you.

F. Watch for customers who pretend not to know each other, but who keep exchanging glances.

Action

Ideally, there should be two or more defenders. A basic tactic is never to bunch up in one spot, which would allow one robber the opportunity to cover all of them with his weapon. Keeping apart makes it difficult to watch each one closely. If there are two or more robbers, the defenders will each take the ones nearest to him. The signal to open fire comes only from the owner or manager. It's not verbal. The others just keep their eyes on him and follow his lead.

An important consideration is whether other people are on the premises at the time. If any innocent people are endangered, it's better to give the robber what he wants. If there were a shoot-out, an innocent person hit by the robber's gunfire could try to sue the business owner on the grounds that if he had not resisted, the shooting would not have started.

Stake-out

If your business is in a high-crime area, you might consider a stake-out. This would be with the help of other businessmen. For this, an initial meeting can lay the groundwork. This would settle two important points, the first being whether it's advisable to take direct action, or leave the matter to the police. Often, the police don't have the manpower for intensive protection, and the citizen and businessman are left on their own.

The second point concerns the law. Stake-outs by civilians may be illegal in that jurisdiction. An ambitious prosecutor may label your group *vigilante* and try to grab headlines by action against you. If this is the case, get competent legal advice from the right sort of lawyer.

A lawyer who limits his advice to reciting the law and telling you to stay within it isn't worth much. The sort of attorney you need is the kind who helps you to do what you want, yet avoid prosecution. This isn't immoral. People and companies bend the law every day. Some break it. Among those who break the law most conspicuously are armed robbers.

A good attorney will help you slip through the rough spots after a shooting, too. In this regard, be very sure that you have his home number, so that you can reach him after-hours as well. Being able to summon legal advice quickly can make the aftermath of a shooting much less stressful.

Once you and your fellow businessmen feel that you can proceed without sanctions from the law, you may decide which business to stake out. The answer's usually self-evident, the one which has been robbed most often.

Physical preparations are similar to those for normal armed defense, but more elaborate because there are more resources available. In some cases, it's worth the trouble to cut an extra door to the back room to allow the stake-out team quicker access. Another way is to install one-way mirrors, or light curtains, through which members of the team can scrutinize store customers. The arrangement is to catch the robber or robbers in a cross-fire. If team members inside aren't enough for this, there can be others hidden next door. Another concern is stopping the get-away. It's illegal to open fire to prevent escape, but disabling a get-away vehicle is a better choice.

How many people up front? The answer should be "As few as possible." Having fewer people minimizes the risk to those in the line of fire. It also simplifies the plan. Unless the stake-out is during a peak period, one person at the counter is enough.

Robberies don't often happen during peak periods. As we've seen, robbers prefer to strike when nobody else is on the premises. During these slow periods, often during the hours of darkness, one person should be able to handle the store, and present a vulnerable appearance to a potential robber.

All members of the stake-out team should plan and rehearse before they expect to go into action. It's important to decide what to do if there are innocent people in the store as well as the robber. Signals are essential. The person in front must be able to alert the backroom team if he notices anything suspicious.

A series of rehearsals will be worthwhile because they'll reveal unforeseen hitches in the plan. Plans rarely work out exactly as devised, and rehearsals will show the need for flexibility and a set of standby tactics.

Robbers, if they're "pros," will have rehearsed their plan. They may profit from the experience of having worked together through several jobs. This works in their favor. However, you and your team can regain the advantage because you'll have rehearsed on your own ground and the robbers won't have.

Deterrent

The advantage of capturing or shooting it out with a robber in the workplace is that you and your fellow businessmen can build up reputations that will deter some hoods who hear of it. Career criminals, and even amateurs, tend to prefer soft targets. The hard, well-protected, and thereby more risky target is one they prefer not to approach.

BE PREPARED

In the Old West, shopkeepers expected occasional armed robberies, and prepared accordingly. Unfortunately, the picture hasn't improved over that of the Old West, and today's businessman must anticipate a greater variety of dangers.

PERSONAL SECURITY OUTDOORS

You may fortify your home or workplace, but you can't remain there 24 hours a day. When you commute or travel for personal reasons or pleasure, you're beyond your immediate protection. Some locales are extremely dangerous. In some cities, acting paranoid, as if everyone who approaches is "out to get you," is merely hard-core realism. Some areas are so dangerous that even police officers only enter in pairs. The *safer* areas aren't entirely safe, as two-footed predators often seek their prey there.

Let's consider how to promote personal safety in several everyday situations and activities. In all situations, it's important to keep alert and watch for warning signs of danger. Along with alertness, never assume anything or any situation is safe until you've checked it out.

WALKING

When walking in the street keep clear of places that might conceal an attacker. Keep away from dark doorways. Also walk wide around corners to reduce the risk of being grabbed by anyone lurking behind the corner. Remember that a line of parked cars can conceal an attacker.

The risk varies with the area and the time. Avoid the riskiest areas and the hours of darkness if you can. If you're a businessman taking the day's receipts to the bank, it's smart to avoid doing it at the end of the day. Choose the late afternoon when there are heavy crowds on the street.

Be aware of people around and behind you. In a crowd, it's not possible to detect a tail easily, but the risk of robbery in a crowd is less. On a deserted street, anyone shadowing you will be more conspicuous.

One of the danger signs is people who don't belong. This can mean juveniles in a retirement community, or people dressed very differently from most others.

Other danger signs have to do with cars. Cars that seem to be cruising slowly, cars you see going around the block several times, and cars that seem out of place are all suspicious. A parked car with one or more occupants can be a danger sign. In this regard, it's vital to know the characteristics of the area. On the "strip," a parked car with a male occupant may simply be a potential client looking for a prostitute. The man can also be a vice squad officer looking for a "bust." Drug dealers and their clients also show loitering behavior, but only in the agreed-upon selling areas.

Beware of strangers who approach and speak to you. The approach may be totally innocent, but it also may be a set-up for a mugging or a distraction for pocket-picking if it takes place in a crowd. The first step upon being approached is to do a half-turn to the side. This allows you to face the person at an angle.

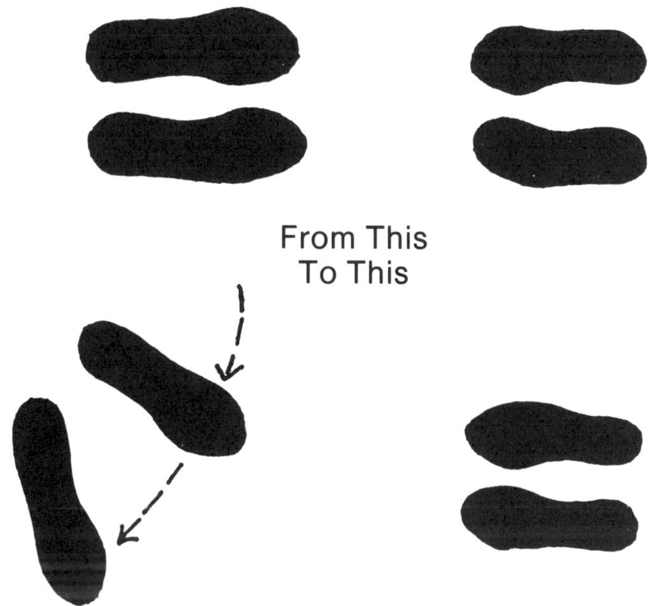

Shifting the feet to face the other person at an angle allows you to get into a defensive position. You may have noticed that police officers usually adopt this stance when interviewing people on the street. If you're right-handed, and your weapon's on your right side, turn your left side towards the person you're facing. If you're left-handed, do the reverse. This keeps your weapon farthest from an attacker. You use the off-hand for defense, blocking or parrying blows, while drawing your weapon with your strong hand.

Turning also allows a quick look to the rear and the side, in case another person's converging on you. Be prepared to move quickly. If you see an attack coming, it's morally justifiable to attack them first.

If you keep the weapon in your pocket, walk with your hands in your pockets.

When entering an elevator, look for blind spots that might conceal an attacker. Look in the upper corners, as many elevators have mirrors for this purpose. When leaving an elevator, take similar precautions, as muggers sometimes wait on the ground floor or the garage floor. In some areas, truly strange things happen. A woman getting out of an elevator in a Manhattan Welfare Center walked right into a dangerous scene involving an angry welfare client, with a can of lye, who was dousing anyone he saw. It's also possible to walk into a stick-up, if the elevator doors open up into a bank or jewelry store. This is also true if taking a short-cut, such as the fire stairs. Startling an armed robber can be very dangerous, and result in a shooting.

Two pairs of hands, and eyes are better than one. In dangerous areas, you'd be better off with a companion.

When entering strange rooms, places where you don't normally go, you need to take special precautions. Try to know who or what is inside before you enter. Check the place out through a window or an open doorway. This is especially easy on the subway, as you should consider a subway car as a "strange room." The many large windows in subway cars allow you to scan the full length. This is important to do even during the rush hour, because there might be a knife-wielding maniac hacking at anyone within reach.

Public toilets can be very dangerous, depending on the locale. Those in some city parks and some theaters can be havens for perverts, who are relatively harmless, or for muggers. Occasionally, there will be a mugger masquerading as a pervert, enticing people to accompany him to a place where he can mug them with more privacy.

A public toilet in an airport is usually safer than one in a bus depot. Any toilet with heavy traffic is probably safer than one with only an occasional client. If you enter one with only a single occupant, be alert, even if all you see is a pair of feet under a stall door. Keep a lookout in the mirror, or keep your head turned, because the person might be a mugger waiting for prey.

SUBWAYS

In some cities, such as Washington, D.C., subways are fast, efficient, and clean. In New York, they're awful, so bad that the city government has had to give its tacit approval to a vigilante group, the *Guardian Angels,* to patrol the subways because the police can't cope.

If you're forced to ride the subway late at night, take special precautions. Even if the car's deserted, you don't know who will get on at the next station. Don't, above all, fall asleep in the subway. You may never wake up. One way to avoid falling asleep is to keep on your feet, but sometimes even this doesn't work. Subway travelers know that some subway riders can sleep on their feet. As a last resort, get off the train and get a cup of coffee from a vending machine or an all-night diner.

Inter-urban trains are not in the same class as subways. Normal precautions are usually all you need.

Watch your luggage, and if you have a compartment, lock the door. Simple and inexpensive travel locks are commonly available, and will prevent anyone from entering your compartment, even with a key.

AIRLINES

The electronic checks at terminals make it difficult for anyone to smuggle a firearm on board, but you ought to be aware that many of them don't work adequately. This was one of the major news stories of 1987.

If you have any doubts about the effectiveness of the weapons detection procedures at your local airport, carry a briefcase with a heavy stapler with you, and see if you get stopped. If a staple gun passes the electronic check and the X-ray, a firearm may, also.

Terminals are well-policed, but one danger is that someone might steal your luggage off the carousel. If you see someone else pick up your luggage, you usually have one supreme advantage. Unless he's been stalking you, he doesn't know what you look like. You can follow him until you find a police officer, or come to a place where you can recover your luggage by force.

You ought to be aware of a few weapons which will easily pass the security checks, and which people *can* smuggle aboard an airliner. One is a club, made of wood or plastic. A leather blackjack will also pass, unless it's filled with lead powder. A glass fiber knife, weighing about an ounce, is also easy to bring aboard. Plastic explosive will not set off the detectors. All of these can be used by "skyjackers," and if you're on an aircraft being skyjacked, you're in more trouble than you can handle.

Avoiding trouble is the best way to go. Certain airlines, such as El-Al and others operated by countries which are controversial, are constant targets. If it's not a skyjacker, it's a missile fired from near the airport runway. The headlines will tell you which airlines are having spates of problems, and staying off their aircraft is the safest course for you.

TAKEN HOSTAGE

This can happen anywhere. The airline hostages make the most headlines, but if you happen to be in the middle of an interrupted robbery the stick-up artist might hold you and others hostage. This is an unusually grim situation because you may have more to fear from the police than from the suspect.

If the suspect intended to kill you, you'd already be dead. Only live hostages are worth anything. To the police, however, hostages are nuisances, and very expendable. Many S.W.A.T. officers feel it's better to let hostages die than to let felons escape. They also prefer to show other criminals that taking hostages won't do them any good in the end. In some cases, police will agree to letting the suspect leave, but will open fire on him when they get a clear shot. This is what happened in Beverly Hills in 1986 when a Los Angeles County S.W.A.T. sniper shot the jewelry store manager instead of the suspect. He'd been given the wrong description.

If you're taken hostage, try to escape if you can. You may find a rear exit, or be able to crawl out of a bathroom window. If you can't get away, remember that the longer you're held captive, the more likely it becomes that a S.W.A.T. team will come crashing in. Pick out some cover and prepare to dive for it when things start happening. Here's what you can expect:

1. A loud explosion will be the "explosive entry." Police knock the door down with explosives. They also may blow a hole in a wall.

2. Loud noises and bright flashes are "stun grenades," to temporarily incapacitate anyone inside. These may dazzle you, rupture your eardrums, and cause nosebleeds. Some spray burning magnesium and can cause severe burns.

3. The entry team comes in, prepared to shoot any suspects. Actually, they'll shoot anyone they see with a weapon. This is why you should not try to disarm any suspects when the police attack. They'll take you for a suspect and blow you away without discussion or hesitation. They are also prepared to blow away anyone who may appear threatening, and this can mean anyone still standing. Just dive for cover and lie still.

AUTOMOBILE TRAVEL

Many crimes involve automobiles, and the picture's getting worse. One reason is that Americans spend a lot of time in cars. Cars also facilitate certain types of crimes that require fast transportation.

The precautions you choose to take will depend on the area in which you live. If you live in California, with its freeway shootings, you may wish you had a tank. With all that, you ought to recognize one fundamental fact, you're far safer in your car than alone on foot. You can lock yourself in a glass and steel box that will impede access to you, which can get you out of danger very quickly, and which can also serve as a very deadly weapon.

Today, all cars have locks. Make use of them. Lock your car when you park it. In some parts of the country, this is a useless precaution, but in others it can be a life-saver. Locking the car is not to keep it from being stolen, as a professional car thief can get through the lock in a couple of seconds. The point is to keep anyone from hiding inside it, waiting for your return.

Alarms aren't as useful as their makers claim. There are alarms with trembler switches that set off the gong when anyone touches your car. This can be a nuisance in a crowded area, where people are walking by and bumping against your car constantly.

Before unlocking your car, look inside, in both front and back seats, to make sure there's nobody waiting. If you see anyone, either call the police or back off to a safe distance with your weapon ready, and order the intruder out.

Keep the doors locked while driving. This isn't very important on highways, but in city traffic some muggers jump into cars pausing for stop signs and red lights.

Don't pick up hitchhikers. Ten or twenty years ago, it was still safe in many parts of the country, but no more. Today, violence is only one potential problem.

Picking up a minor who then tries to extort money from you with a false accusation of "rape" or "molesting" is equally possible.

Be alert when you drive. Traffic conditions can be dangerous, but there's also possible danger from people approaching your car. Watch for blocked streets, or obstacles that force you to slow down and stop, especially on an uncrowded road. You should "drive ahead of your car," both to avoid traffic accidents and to avoid ambushes.

Local conditions change with the time of day. The business district, crowded with people during the day, becomes very lonely at night. In some areas, street people come out at night and turn the streets into jungles.

If you're packing a gun, don't wear it when driving. Most holsters don't allow quick draw from a seated position. Lay the weapon on the seat next to you.

Another precaution is to wear an armored vest if you have to drive in a risky area. Your car won't necessarily stop bullets, and in some cases a vest might be a wise step.

As when walking, having a partner more than doubles your defensive power. Having a companion *riding shotgun* means an extra pair of eyes to scan for trouble. As the driver, your attention's always divided. Your passenger can scan ahead and behind, giving his full attention to anything that threatens your security.

ENCOUNTERS

If you run into a problem, try to drive out of it, rather than stay and fight it out. Often, what looks like a very threatening situation can only become worse if you stay. Your car can take you out of a trap very quickly, and this must be your first choice. With the doors locked, it isn't easy for anyone to drag you out of your car, even if you're stopped. However, if you stay in place, a club or tire iron can smash a window.

Don't hesitate to run down any attacker physically blocking your path. If this is the only way to escape, do it. It may seem more manly to stand and fight, but it's smart to get away.

Your car is a lethal weapon. Remember that it can hit with tens or hundreds of thousands of pounds of kinetic energy. Even a rifle bullet, typically, has only a couple of thousand pounds of kinetic energy. Ramming sometimes is the best way to go. Let's calculate why.

An attacker jumps into the road, pointing a weapon at you and waving you down. If he's 40 feet away, and you're driving at 30 miles per hour, you're covering 44 feet in one second. If you don't spend much time in thinking about it, you can grab a weapon from the seat and raise it in a second. Hitting from a moving car while driving with one hand is another matter. Accelerating and running him down takes less than a second. If your attacker understands what you intend in time to jump out of the way, he won't be able to fire very effectively while he's jumping to save his life. By the time he recovers, you'll be hundreds of yards down the road.

If you see the attacker far enough ahead that you could stop, draw your weapon, and open fire effectively, you probably have enough room to turn around. If the road's too narrow, drop into reverse gear.

If you're driving with the window open, you're increasing your vulnerability. If you stop for a light, anyone can reach in and grab you. If this happens, the best defense is to step on the gas hard, even if he has a solid grip on you. Once he's swept off his feet, his grip will loosen quickly. If you feel vindictive, you can grab his hand and drag him with you until you get up to over 60 miles per hour, and let go. Doing this will prevent him from victimizing other motorists for a long time.

If the attacker has a grip on you and doesn't let go, the only way left to break him loose is to sideswipe a wall or another vehicle. At this point, don't worry about the damage to your car. Your life's at stake. You also need not worry too much about explanations to the police. You simply state, if you should decide to report it, that you drove off to escape and that the thug held on too long.

The next way to beat off an attack is by gunfire. With a weapon on the seat next to you, bringing it into play won't take long. If you have a partner, this gives you a crucial "edge" over the attacker because he can't watch you both.

Shooting inside a car poses a couple of problems. One is noise. You'd be surprised how loud gunfire sounds inside a car. If you startle easily, you may jump out of your shoes the first time you hear a weapon discharged inside a car. The other point is always fire from inside a car if you can. Don't get out to shoot. This deprives you of some protection, and it'll take you longer to drive away if you suddenly find that you need to.

If there's more than a single attacker, shoot it out with the closest one as you drive away. This is the smart tactic. It's bad tactics to stay if you're outnumbered. Even if there are two of you, with one driving and one shooting, it's better to drive off than to stay.

Shooting from a moving vehicle is risky. Unless you've practiced and are good at it, you'll probably miss. Be especially careful if there are innocent people in view. This isn't too likely, because an attack will probably take place in a lonely area.

EVADING PURSUIT

Gunfire is very effective in discouraging pursuit, but it's not the only way. It may actually be the least desirable way. Trying to hit a following car can be next to impossible, especially when driving over a rough road. If you have to drive and shoot, it's hopeless.

A better way is to gain a slight lead, then stop and take cover at the side of the road, opening fire when the pursuer comes into effective range. In this case, effective range means when you don't have to lead your target to compensate for his speed. If you're close to roadside, he'll be coming almost directly at you, and you can aim straight on, without having to worry about lead.

There's only one truly good way to discourage pursuit. This is stopping it cold by causing a collision. You need about a minute's lead time for this, enough to get around a corner or bend and to place an obstacle in the road where the pursuer can't avoid it or crashes into a solid object while trying to steer out of it. Anything can be an obstacle; a log, rocks, even a car seat. An empty garbage can will do because the oncoming driver won't be able to tell that it's empty. As a last resort, place your car in the middle of the road and, after the crash, open fire on any survivors.

Some situations don't justify gunfire at all. You may be pursued by someone whom you cut off inadvertently in traffic. He might be honking his horn at you, or flashing his bright lights into your mirror at night. You don't really want an altercation with him, and you're trying to get him off your tail without violence.

On a freeway, one way is to wait until you're right next to an exit, cut your wheel hard, and take the exit too late for him to follow you. This requires that there be enough of a gap so that you don't cut anyone else off when you do this. The technique works best, however, if your pursuer is pulling up on your left side to curse you out. When you cut your wheel, you'll swing away from him too quickly for him to recover and cross both lanes to take the exit.

In city streets, evading pursuit requires that you gain a lead on your pursuer. If you can gain about 50 yards, this is enough for you to take a corner quickly, pull over to the curb, and stop. Cut your engine and lights, and lay down on the seat. Another choice is to cut your lights and go down an alley to the next street. Under no circumstances should you enter an alley or driveway with no exit. This would trap you.

SHOOTING IT OUT

If you're forced to stop, and you have to use your car for cover as you shoot to save your life, use good tactics for survival. Always try to park your car at an angle to the threat.

If you're alone, pull over to the left and dive out the driver's door. Use the engine compartment as cover. If you have a partner, pull over to the right. Your partner dives out of his door while you lay down flat on the seats. Follow him out the right-hand door as soon as he's clear. Your partner goes back to fire over or around the rear deck, while you use the engine compartment for a shield. The rear deck will work for cover because bullets have to penetrate a door, the rear seat, and the trunk to get to anyone sheltering behind it. However, the car must be angled for this to work. Bullet-holes will, however, spoil its trade-in value. This is a good point to remember if you get involved in a shoot-out in the street. Use somebody else's car for cover if you can.

When using the car as cover, remember not to rest the weapon on the car. It's slower if you do, and you can waste a second or two getting into position. Stay a couple of feet behind it, and pop up to fire. This isn't as steady, but it's a lot faster.

WALK AWAY

As we've discussed earlier, the police may treat you as a suspect, not as a hero.

If you get into an affray outside of your premises, you may have the choice of walking away. Because thugs prefer to work when there are no witnesses, you may be able to leave the scene without being stopped or questioned. The harrowing experience of Bernard Goetz teaches us all a lesson on the value of discretion. Staying to offer explanations to the police can be a losing game.

If your decision is to walk away, get your priorities straight. If there are people nearby who may have heard the affray and reported it to the police, you may have to leave very quickly. If you have a minute or two, you might look for any ejected shells if you've been using an auto pistol. Also check the area for anything you may have dropped. Then leave, don't look back, and don't tell anyone of the affair.

GUNPOINT

When confronting a felon, you'll have to decide at some point whether you shoot or not. If you have to shoot, the urgency will be so great that you won't have time to deliberate for long. Although the decision to open fire is the most serious one you'll have to make, it's possible to pre-program it so that your reaction time is minimal. This is necessary because when you're facing an armed and dangerous suspect, hesitation could cost you your life. It's also possible to manage the confrontation to give you more time to decide.

Let's discuss some aspects of a shooting decision so that you may plan the best course for yourself.

MAKING A DECISION

Deadly Threat

If your suspect is a deadly threat to you and your family, not shooting can bring very serious consequences. Evaluating whether he is or not depends on the situation. You may see that he's armed, or the circumstances may be such that you can't afford to wait to find out. A night intruder in your home, for example, is a threatening figure even if unarmed. The darkness makes it difficult to determine if he is, and the safest course is to open fire.

Warning

In many cases, a verbal warning will stop the attack or intrusion. Whether you want to try this depends on how you see the threat. If you see no evidence of a weapon, and the intruder doesn't seem to be very aggressive, you may want to risk a warning, with the understanding that if he resists you'll fire.

The warning you give depends on the situation and how close the intruder is to you. On your property, if he's outside and you're inside, you can take cover and train your weapon on him. You then announce that you have him covered, and that he's to get off your property. Ordering him to leave is the safest course if he's outside, because if you try to hold him for the police and he runs, you can't shoot. If you try to bring him inside, you're courting danger.

If the suspect's inside, you may choose to yell "*Freeze,*" and to fire if he doesn't. The danger here is that there's probably not much space between you and him. He may be close enough to rush you. If you can see that the suspect is armed you may decide to open fire without warning. This is the safest course.

The Confrontation

When the moment comes, you have to think quickly. Most of this will be subconscious, if you've planned well and made your basic decisions ahead of time. Let's take a hypothetical robbery as an example. This may happen on the street, in a store, on the subway, or even in your home.

To use the correct tactical building blocks, you have to assess your opponent and assess the situation. You have to observe if he's armed, and if so, with what? How close is he? Does he have accomplices? What sort of person does he seem to be? A thrill killer? A robber?

If there's more than one attacker, it can be a very bad situation with no hope of a counter-move if the assailants are street savvy. Not all of them are, though. Good tactics for them means covering you from different angles and staying out of each other's line of fire.

You then have to examine your situation. Are you alone? Armed? Can you get your weapon into action before he can hurt you? How desperate are you, anyway? Do you have a family to protect? Is help nearby?

If you decide to fold, that's it. You cooperate and hope that he'll take what he wants and leave. If you decide to resist, you must choose your moment.

There's a certain timing to a confrontation. Knowing this means you can use it to your advantage.

The first beat is the facing down. The robber or mugger accosts you, displays his weapon, makes his demand, and waits for your reaction. Then you respond, either by giving in or by defiance. It's during these first two beats that the robber is most alert, sizing you up, waiting for a sign of what you're going to do.

It's during this time that you have to put him off his guard. Don't try to act tough. Look and sound meek. Say you don't want trouble. Act scared. Wait for the moment.

It can help to whine and beg. Tell him not to hurt you because your 88-year old mother needs you. The more spineless you appear, the less reason he has to be wary.

Distraction

The moment for a counter-move is when his full attention isn't on you. As long as his mind is on you, he's waiting for you to make a false move. He's got his own mental trigger. Distracting him, even for a moment, can unhook his mental trigger. If someone else comes on the scene, he'll have to focus his attention on that person and assess the potential threat. You can also create the moment.

One way is to drop your wallet when you hand it over. He's not going to bend over unless he's awfully stupid. However, the moment he takes to think the situation over can give you a chance if you're close enough to go for his weapon hand while you draw your own.

The counter-attack makes it or breaks it right there. Either you're successful or you're dead or severely injured, and it happens fast. This is why your priorities have to be clear. They are first, to protect yourself, and secondly, to neutralize him.

"Beating the drop" is the term used for drawing your weapon before your attacker can fire his. It may be possible if he's very slow in his reflexes, but normally you'll have to do something else to help.

Drawing your weapon quickly isn't the big problem, avoiding harm while doing it is. Much depends on whether or not your robber is in contact range. If he is, deflect his weapon with one hand while drawing yours with the other. Deflecting his weapon is crucial because if you don't he will probably use it on you as you're shooting him. Why?

We have to consider reflexes and reflex time. When facing an armed opponent, you need to put him out of action before he can harm you. Unfortunately, this is very hard to do because there's no such thing as an instantly incapacitating weapon. You can inflict a mortal wound but he'll still have a second or two of consciousness and coordination in which to harm you.

If he's out of reach, your action depends on whether he has a gun, knife, or club. If he's armed with a gun, don't do anything unless you can duck behind cover before he fires. If you feel that he's going to kill you anyway, you can take desperate action. Dive to one side while drawing your weapon and open fire as soon as you're lined up. This gives you a 50-50 chance, whereas before the odds were all in his favor.

If he has a knife or club, and is standing out of reach, you have a better than even chance. Don't be over confident, though. You'd be surprised how quickly an adult male can cross ten feet of space and attack you with a knife.

If there are two attackers, wait to see if one blocks the other's line of fire when he approaches you. The closer one may even put away his weapon if he's going to "shake you down." This gives you an opening. Grab him and use him as a shield while you draw and fire. Shoot him first, to prevent his fighting you, then use his body to shield you while you deal with the other. You'll find your clothes covered with blood after it's over, but this isn't as bad as if the blood were your own.

In some situations, you might decide to delay your response. The odds may just not be that good while he's training his weapon on you.

The moment he prepares to leave is critical. This is when you find out for sure whether he intends to eliminate anyone who might identify him. He might prefer to tie you up, or simply to slug you. If so, he'll have to approach, which gives you an opening.

When he turns to make his escape, you might be tempted to draw and fire. This can get you in hot water, because unless you can demonstrate in court that the fleeing felon was endangering someone else when you shot him, you'll be charged with murder or manslaughter.

Whatever you do, avoid pursuing him with a weapon in your hand. Police officers tend to open fire on anyone they see running with a gun. Businessmen chasing robbers have been killed this way.

If you have to pursue, do it by car. This gives you the speed advantage, and you can keep a weapon on the seat next to you without risking getting shot by the police. Be aware, though, that if you get into an accident during the pursuit you're legally liable. This is why your best tactic is to hang back and hope that the fleeing suspect remains unaware of your pursuit. Don't try to stop him yourself, but look for a police patrol and advise them of the situation.

CAPTURE

Let's consider trying to take the suspect alive and turning him over to the police. Although this may seem to be a fairly conservative action, consider what you face before making the final decision. If the intruder fails to obey your order to freeze, and fires at you, his shots may endanger your family as well as yourself. You also give up the tactical advantage of surprise. If he appears to comply, then goes for a weapon, you'll be caught short.

Be extremely careful in approaching the suspect. Closer than ten feet, you're in deadly danger if he decides to come for you. If he's skilled in unarmed combat, he may disarm you before you can react. Never lose sight of the fact that he's "street-smart" and you're not. Also consider your age and physical shape compared to his. Do you want to fight him hand-to-hand?

Let's go over the practical aspects of capturing him, once you've made the decision. The first point is that you must be sure that the suspect is alone. If he has a partner whom you haven't spotted, by the time you find out it'll be too late.

Controlling The Suspect

Yell *Freeze* from behind cover. This protects you in case he opens fire. Cover also blocks him in case he decides to rush you. Also watch for the suspect who eases up on you. This is the "salami-slicing" technique, with the suspect edging up on you in very small steps. All the while, he'll be talking to distract you, hoping that you won't notice the danger until it's too late. This is a very effective technique because the threat is creeping. It's hard to draw the line and decide, "This far, and no more."

This is the crucial point where a mental trigger is necessary. You should have nothing on your mind but "If he makes the wrong move, I'll shoot." Also decide how close he may come before you fire. Ten feet should be the absolute minimum, but many rooms don't afford that much space. This is why you should think of controlling the situation from the next room.

Don't let him speak. If he tries to say anything to you, it can divide your attention and make you vulnerable to a disarming tactic. The street-wise preliminary to a disarm is to distract the subject by asking him a question. It's very important to remember this if you decide to approach him. You're set up with a mental trigger, and you must keep your attention on it. If the suspect succeeds in distracting you, you'll have your mind "uncocked" and may not be able to react quickly enough if he makes a hostile move.

If the room lights aren't on, turn them on. Remain in the shadows and behind cover until you've thoroughly evaluated the situation. If he's holding a weapon, tell him to place it on the ground. Don't tell him to "drop it." This can result in an accidental discharge. If he has nothing in his hands, have him hold his hands on top of his head with fingers laced. Have him turn around slowly so that you may look him over for bulges which may hide a gun.

The next step is to "prone him out." First, have him face away from you. This is important because it puts him at a disadvantage. You must always keep him under close scrutiny, but not let him know exactly where you are, for your own safety.

Tell him to drop to one knee, then the other. Next, have him place both hands on the floor in front of him, and to let himself down until he's flat, still facing away from you. Have him place his arms out to his sides, palms up.

Searching The Suspect

At this point, you may be satisfied to keep the suspect under control and call the police. If someone else can handle the phone, you can keep the suspect safely under control. If you're alone, you'll have to do both. If the phone's in the same room, the problem is simply keeping your eye on the suspect while you make the call. Make sure that you tell the police that you're holding the suspect at gunpoint. Give the dispatcher your description and the suspect's.

If the phone's in another room and you're alone with the suspect, you have two choices. One is to move the suspect. Tell him to crawl where you direct. A way to reduce the chances of his jumping up for a surprise attack is to order him to drop his pants down to his ankles. The other way is to immobilize him after a search.

There are two safe ways to go about searching him. Neither is the way you see on TV, with the suspect leaning on a car or wall. The first is with the suspect prone. You approach from the rear or side, so that he can't see you. Order him to place one ankle behind his knee. Grab his other ankle and bring it up to lock his ankle behind the knee. This is how you control him. He can't move much with the leg-lock on him, and you can cause him pain by applying pressure.

At this point you will have to holster your weapon or put it in a pocket. Do this only when you're sure that you have the suspect under control with the leg-lock. It's also important to keep the suspect from seeing that you no longer have a weapon in your hand. Keep him facing away from you.

Search his legs first, paying special attention to the ankles where a knife or small gun might be tucked into the sock. Once you're sure his ankles and calves are clean, you may straddle his upper ankle. Letting your weight down hard on it will cause him pain. This is how you keep him under control and your hands free for the rest of the search. An additional control technique you can use when you have to move up his body is to grab one of his hands and bend a finger back. Pressure against the finger joint can cause intense pain, and serves as a control technique.

Work up to his thighs, then his crotch. It's at this point that a street-wise suspect may try to fake you out. If he has a weapon hidden in the crotch area, he may say something like: "Hey, getting your rocks off, feeling me up?" Don't let this intimidate you. Just tell him to shut up. Continue the search, and work your way up to his waist.

If you have handcuffs, you may find this the best moment to put them on. A quick improvisation if you lack hand-cuffs is super glue. A few drops on his hands will glue them together so that he can't release them. Acetone will remove the super glue when necessary.

If you can't do either, make sure the suspect keeps his arms out to his sides, palms up. The finger-bend control technique comes in handy here. Continue to search his upper body, paying attention to the armpits. Have him shift slightly so that you can search the front of his chest and his abdomen. Search his neck, watching for anything on a cord or chain. Some street maggots carry knives on a string or chain around the neck. Run your hands through his hair.

If the suspect is wounded when you approach for a search, first determine if he can hear you, or whether he's unresponsive. Remember that he may be faking it. Approach him from his blind side. If he still has a weapon in his hand, get control of the weapon first. Remove it. If it's near his hand, remove it or kick it away. Order him to cross his legs. If he doesn't respond, grab his ankle, and place it on the other knee. Retain control this way and start to search him.

A critical point is never to assume that the suspect has only one weapon. Don't stop searching after finding a weapon. Remember that knives can be very small. A single-edged razor blade is very flat. This is why it's a good idea to run your hand flat along his clothing to feel for bulges, then go back and crumple it to feel for hard objects.

The second method is the strip-search. This is extremely safe because you don't have to approach the suspect. You may wish to do this if you're in a remote area and alone with the suspect. If the suspect is much larger than you, there's a real danger that he might roll over, even with your sitting on his ankle, and overpower you during a search. The strip-search lets you take his weapons away without endangering yourself, at a slight risk that he'll get his hands close to a weapon and try to use it.

To conduct a strip-search properly, first prone him out and have him face away from you. Stay behind cover while he's moving. When he's proned out to your satisfaction, order him to take his clothes off, and to throw everything away from his body. Make it clear that any false move will be a signal for you to fire. Once you see him start, quietly change your position. If he's planning to go for a gun and fire at you, he only knows where you are by the sound of your voice, and he'll fire in the wrong direction.

ESCAPE

Sometimes, it's better to let a suspect escape than risk capturing him and having to handle an unwilling captive. In certain circumstances, you really have no choice. If he doesn't freeze when you order him, but takes off in the opposite direction, you'll have a hard time explaining to the police and to a jury why you shot him in the back. If you come upon a burglar, you can't use deadly force to prevent his stealing your property.

THE ALIBI WEAPON

There has been little hard information about the "alibi gun," "throw-down knife," and other weapons used to justify a shooting after the fact. We find very little written about alibi weapons for obvious reasons. Those with first-hand experience are reluctant to set down their views in black-and-white. Police officers who do write about this touchy topic tend to denounce the practice. What else can they do? If they wrote of alibi guns approvingly, it would be a reflection upon their departments. We ought to study the subject to clear the air. The purpose is not to encourage you to employ an alibi weapon, but to inform you of the facts, and to suggest techniques to avoid accidental and unjustified shootings.

The "alibi gun" is a small, cheap handgun used to cover an unjustified shooting. Bill Jordan, formerly an Inspector with the U.S. Border Patrol, presents a good picture of how an alibi gun can serve to clear an officer from a charge of wrongful shooting.[1] He describes how an officer had shot a suspect without finding a handgun on his body. The shooting took place on a bridge, and Jordan tells how he went to the scene and deposited a handgun of the proper description in the water. When investigators used an electro-magnet to retrieve the alleged weapon, the magnet came up with several stuck to it. Jordan shows that, in human terms, illegally placing an alibi gun is very understandable. Let's note, however, that Jordan did not write about this subject until after he'd retired from his agency.

It's easy for a police officer to obtain a weapon that can't be traced to him. When he shakes down a street hood and finds a weapon, he can simply take it. If weapon possession or concealed carry are illegal, the suspect will be happy to have the officer keep it and not press a weapon charge on him.

Civilians have only a slightly harder time of it. Often, a handgun or knife is easily found at a garage sale. An important point is that the weapon doesn't have to be real. There have been several mistaken shootings in which the victim was armed with a real-looking toy gun. Keeping the object in a plastic bag is one way of avoiding a last minute rush to erase fingerprints.

PREVENTING ACCIDENTAL SHOOTINGS

Accidental shootings happen. Sometimes the finger is too tight on the trigger during a stressful moment and there's an accidental discharge. This is why it's important never to hold anyone at gunpoint with a cocked revolver. It needs only light pressure on the trigger to fire. With a modern auto pistol, use the decocking lever, if it has one, to bring the hammer down from full cock.

It's also wise to be sure of your target. Using night lights to identify your target, or at least to be sure that it's nobody you know, is a good precaution. Finally, don't be in a hurry to shoot. If you understand and practice good tactics you won't need an alibi gun. Staying behind cover gives you the time to make a valid "shoot/don't shoot" decision.

SUSPECT HANDLING IS VITAL

Understanding the basics of suspect handling is critically important because you will have to cope with close confrontations. You'll also need to know this to avoid being victimized when trying to save a suspect for trial.

NOTES

1. *No Second Place Winner,* Bill Jordan, Shreveport, LA, Privately Printed, 1965, pp. 15-17.

GETTING HELP FROM OFFICIAL PROGRAMS

Many police departments have introduced various crime prevention and crime reduction programs. These allow citizens to feel that they're doing something worthwhile to protect themselves and their property. Some of these programs have a few positive values:

Operation Identification involves marking valuable property with an engraving tool. With your social security number or driver's license number on everything valuable you own, subsequent identification in case of recovery is easier. You also record a description and the serial number, if any, on a form provided by the police. The police provide stickers and decals to put on your doors and windows.

The identification numbers are valuable only if the police recover your stolen property. It will speed your getting it back. The good news is that the stickers seem to deter burglars. Homes without stickers get burglarized between 40 and 100 times as often as those with the *Operation Identification* decals, depending on the community. This suggests that the best and most cost-effective method is putting the stickers on your home.

There are several types of *Blockwatch* programs across the country. Some are called *PACE* (People's Anti-Crime Effort) and *Neighborhood Watch.* They all work about the same way. Police organize meetings and show films on home security. They encourage residents to keep their eyes and ears open and to report any suspicious activity. They emphasize that citizens are not to take action themselves but to let the police handle it. The success of these programs depend on the response time of the police.

A very valuable aspect of these programs is that some police departments will send an officer to your home to conduct a security survey, and point out weaknesses that a burglar might exploit. This is a point to watch, because there's less chance of a criminal prying a weapon out of your cold, dead fingers than of lifting it from your house while you're not at home.

LEGAL PROBLEMS

In shooting to survive, you can "win the war," yet lose the peace. Sometimes a citizen acts in what he thinks is self-defense and finds himself being prosecuted. This can happen through an error of judgment or ignorance of the law.

A DIFFERENT WORLD

If ever you're in a shoot-out, be prepared for a shock. You'll be treated like a suspect, not an honest citizen. The police won't see you as a hero. You'll have to answer many questions many times, and you'll probably come out of it with a very different viewpoint on the police and our society. Even if you're fully justified, the best you can expect is a searching investigation.

KNOW THE LAWS

The logical first step for you is to inform yourself of the laws in your area. Let's outline the general principles of the laws regarding deadly force, with the understanding that not all states have the same laws.

You're justified in using deadly force:

1. To save a life, yours or another's. It has to be a real, physical threat, not a verbal one. An insult or promise of violence isn't enough. The situation must be such that a reasonable person would believe his life was actually in danger.
2. To save yourself or another person from serious bodily harm. This includes rape and all unlawful use of deadly physical force. Generally, the level of response must match the threat. You can't use a gun to defend yourself against a punch.
3. To stop a major crime in progress, such as robbery, rape, arson, kidnaping, etc.

That's it! Anything else exposes you to being charged with manslaughter, or worse.

Police and correctional officers have an additional, and special, justification because of their duties. In some circumstances, they can use deadly force to stop a felon from escaping. This course is not open to civilians under any circumstances.

State laws vary in important details. This is why you should check the local laws out very carefully before you decide to act. The local rifle and pistol association can usually advise you. The National Rifle Association can put you in touch with a local club.[1] In some states, you may use deadly force only if you can show that retreat was impossible for you, because you're required to retreat first. Anything else gets you prosecuted. Other states have laws regarding the means of defense, such as gun control laws.

Some states have very harsh laws regarding firearms. New York's "Sullivan Law" is aimed not only at guns, but all manner of concealable weapons. Mere possession is a felony. This was shown by a court decision some years ago regarding what is a concealed weapon. The decision stated that a barber carrying a package of just-purchased straight razors to his barbershop was not violating the intent of the law. The decision clarified the issue, but that such a case ever got to court also says a lot. It means that an innocent man was arrested because he had the tools of his trade on his person. Worse, the District Attorney went along with this idiocy and prosecuted. The barber had to lose time from work and hire a lawyer to defend himself against a charge which should never have been filed.

Another New York case involved a 70-year old man, Morris Green, the victim of a much younger and stronger intruder who broke in and started beating him. Green killed the intruder with an unregistered revolver. This led to a prosecution for Murder One.

According to New York's penal code, any killing during a felony is automatically first-degree murder, even if it's accidental or inadvertent. The intent is that a robber can't claim that his gun went off accidentally. An escaping criminal who kills someone in a traffic accident is also liable. Morris Green's problem was that having an unregistered handgun, even at home, is a felony. When he shot his assailant it became Murder One.

Morris Green's case was not unique. A year later, a young woman attacked by a rapist defended herself with a folding knife she carried in her purse. She wounded the attacker, driving him off, but was charged with a Sullivan Law violation. She could have gone to prison, but fortunately a jury of twelve good men acquitted her. They knew the situation in New York, and had wives and daughters of their own.

Why do these things happen? Combine an overzealous police officer and a prosecutor building his track record with easy convictions and you get cases like these. If you live in such an area, you may be hit with a legal one-two punch that leaves you dazed. The law strikes hard at the ordinary citizen, much harder than it does at the street-wise criminal who knows all the tricks.

SPECIAL CASES

Now let's get to the practical fine points and no-nos. There are a lot of these, and ignoring them can lead you right into a legal booby-trap.

1. Killing or injuring an innocent third person will get you prosecuted, even in a justified shooting. A few states, such as Arizona, have laws absolving the shooter from blame in such circumstances.
2. Some situations, justifying physical force, don't allow deadly force. For example, you can't shoot a trespasser on your property, although you may punch him out in some situations.

This may seem strange, especially to some who have seen the tight security at some government installations. In nuclear arsenals, and on some U.S. Air Force base flight lines, there are signs that read "No Trespassing — Deadly Force Authorized." You have no such privileges. The government can do what it wishes because the government makes the laws.

3. You can't use deadly force in a personal argument, or if you started the affray.
4. You can't counter verbal abuse with physical force of any sort. Even though insulting your wife or mother is a serious breach of courtesy, you can't use it as a defense if you waste someone for it.
5. You may threaten the use of deadly force in defense of property, but you can use it only in defense of your body. You may point a gun at a trespasser or burglar, but you may pull the trigger on him only if there's a real physical threat to yourself. This, however, is a gray area, and there are many ifs, ands, and buts. For example, you can't shoot an assailant armed with a knife if he's fifty feet away. If he edges closer, you can fire when he's a definite threat, which means within about ten or fifteen feet.
6. The level of force must match the situation, and excessive force isn't allowed. If you shoot an attacker, you can't walk over and pump five more shots into his head after he's down. That's execution, and very, very illegal.
7. You must have no reasonable alternative. If time allows, a verbal warning might be appropriate.

8. Never set a booby-trap. This can land you in jail and get you sued in civil court.

Now let's look at some specific examples and see how the various laws apply.

As we've seen, you can't open fire to prevent the escape of a criminal. That means if you see someone running down the street with your TV, you have to catch him and punch him out, because you can't shoot him. If you do, you're in trouble because you can't use deadly force to defend property.

The same goes if you see someone climbing over your patio wall. You can threaten him with a weapon, and order him to leave, but that's it. You can fire only if he comes at you with a weapon.

If you shoot someone inside your home, you can usually justify it by saying that you feared for your life. If it's night, and there's not enough light to see plainly that the intruder's unarmed, the "fear for life" defense will usually work. Don't even mention the two hundred dollars you had in you wallet on the nightstand.

You may have heard the advice: "If you shoot someone outside your house, drag him in before the police come." Surprisingly, even some police officers will advise citizens to do this. It's bad advice. If you drag the person in you're tampering with evidence, which itself is a criminal offense. In any event, it's hard to explain bloodstains outside and a corpse inside.

Warning shots are questionable, and becoming more hazardous to the shooter every year. Many police agencies no longer allow them. The main danger is hitting an innocent person. Firing warning shots also depletes the supply of ammunition in the weapon, a bad tactical move. In some cities, discharging a firearm within city limits is an offense, and an overzealous prosecutor might hit you for this. This is why civilians should not fire any warning shots. If the situation justified deadly force, and a verbal warning doesn't do it, open fire for real.

Some states have a law explicitly allowing deadly force against night intruders without further justification. These laws have picked up the tag "make my day" from the media, but they simplify the defense.

MANEUVERING THROUGH THE LEGAL SYSTEM

If your purpose is survival, the only reasonable viewpoint is: "I'd rather be tried by twelve than carried by six." It's better to face a jury than face the undertaker.

There are a few basics to follow. You need to think about these and make your plans long before it happens. The worst time to plan is on the spot, when you're overwrought and likely to make bad decisions. You need a few basic building blocks of verbal and legal tactics that you can put together to work your way through.

Keep in mind that who you are is as important as what you've done in determining the outcome of a brush with the criminal justice system. Minority group members typically live in high-risk areas, and need a weapon for personal protection more than more affluent citizens in the suburbs. However, who do the police stop and frisk for concealed weapons? Who is likely to make the better impression in court?

After the smoke clears and the police arrive, you'll have to explain what happened. You can't "plead the Fifth" unless you want to appear guilty.

Many people, stunned in the aftershock of a violent affray, will be confused and forget facts. This happens both to victims and those who successfully defended themselves. This is what explains witnesses' contradicting each other. If you've just killed an intruder, the consequences of confusion and telling a bad story to the police can be very serious. The police will take down and examine your statement for grounds for prosecution, your prosecution. Anything you say may be used against you.

This is why you need to have the facts clear in your mind before opening your mouth. What you tell the police must include these basic points:

1. You feared that the suspect was a threat to your life or safety, or that of a third party.
2. The suspect was committing a serious felony.
3. You opened fire to stop him. Never say that you fired to kill him. Killing is not allowed, because of the hypocrisy of our laws, even though it's hard to see how you can stop someone with gunfire without a serious risk of killing him.

This point is so critical that it's worth emphasizing. Never say that four-letter word, "kill," in describing your actions and intentions. Instead, always say "stop."

It also helps if the suspect was armed, or so overpoweringly larger than you as to justify deadly force. Some states have laws that allow "disparity of size" as a justification for deadly force.

Before you say anything to the police, consider whether there are any witnesses who can support or contradict your statement. This can be a double-edged sword. If anyone was with you, be careful that what you say will be consistent with what they'll say. Police often separate witnesses before questioning them, to avoid their comparing accounts, but the police don't always arrive immediately. This allows time to confer.

Keep your story simple. If you're not sure, say so. Simply say "I don't know" or "I'm not sure." Don't allow the police investigator to suggest details to you.

If you're upset, show it. Don't be afraid to show it. It's normal. Also remember that, if you show an unnatural calm, the police will become suspicious and start looking for details to contradict your statement.

It's a mistake to tell too perfect a story. It can seem rehearsed. Don't try to cover all the bases. Above all, don't volunteer anything. Give a simple account of what happened, and let the investigating officer ask about any points that aren't clear.

You should avoid admitting any illegal act, or even suggesting that you might have done anything not 100% legal.

If you're charged, don't go with the public defender. This is usually an inexperienced and over-worked lawyer who tries to dispose of his cases as quickly as possible. He'll advise the quick way out, a plea agreement, even if it's at your expense. "Copping the plea" means admitting guilt in return for a lesser sentence. Why settle for that when you can go to trial and obtain sympathy from the jury?

To defend yourself in a civil or criminal proceeding, you should present a picture of yourself as an upright, respectable citizen, and be prepared to describe the deceased's behavior as violent. It also helps if the suspect acted wildly and irrationally, as if on drugs. Sometimes, the autopsy will reveal alcohol or drugs in the suspect's blood.

IF THE SUSPECT SURVIVES

The only clear advantage if the suspect survives the shooting is that you can't be charged with murder, whatever happens. There are, however, other problems and complications that his living through the experience will bring.

You'll have to testify in court if there's a trial. The suspect may be out on bail, committing other crimes to raise money to pay his lawyer. Criminals have often threatened witnesses, and if your suspect is free, he may decide to try this with you. If he doesn't, his friends might. The police won't do anything to protect you, as assigning a 24-hour bodyguard is too costly. You'll be completely on your own against a street-smart suspect.

Eventual prosecution is uncertain. Criminals sometimes make bail before the arresting officer finishes his report. Suspects also jump bail. Overburdened prosecutors are always ready to deal, offering probation for a guilty plea.

CIVIL LIABILITY

This is a ghastly specter which can haunt you for years after a shooting takes place. If you're lucky enough to live in one of the few states with laws specifically exempting you from civil liability in a justifiable homicide, you won't have to worry about this. In most other states, it's a real threat.

One reason why the threat of civil liability is so dangerous is the nature of civil proceedings. First, any fool can file a lawsuit. That doesn't mean he'll win, but at least he causes you the annoyance and anxiety of hiring a lawyer and formulating a defense.

Another reason is the nature of the proof. Criminal cases require "beyond a reasonable doubt." Civil cases require only "preponderance of evidence." It's easier to win a civil case. One of the people shot in the Bernard Goetz incident on New York's subway has filed a huge lawsuit against Goetz.

A corpse can't sue, but his family and heirs can. Their star witness is dead, but this doesn't necessarily stop a suit.

If this is so, why don't street maggots worry about civil liability? Aren't they equally liable under the law?

They certainly are liable, but they're not as vulnerable as you. You have a steady job, a car, family, and a house. A street thug often only owns the clothes on his back and the needle with which he shoots up. If he has a car legally registered to him, it's either a rolling wreck or he owes many payments on it. Without any real property, or even roots in the community, he has far less to lose than you do. If the going gets too tough, he can quietly slip out of town one night, going beyond the reach of a civil suit.

A MINEFIELD

The legal aftermath of a justified shooting can be very trying. You'll need emotional stamina to see it through, even if you're 100% correct.

NOTES

1. You may contact the National Rifle Association at PO Box 37484, Washington, DC 20013.

THE EMOTIONAL COMPONENT

There's been a lot of writing about post-shooting trauma, a symptom which afflicts police officers after they gun down felons. The theory goes like this: People in our society are raised to be nonviolent, and are taught from an early age that it's wrong to kill. Therefore, when someone is reluctantly forced to take a life, the emotional turmoil this causes can affect his concentration, sleep, sexual potency, and generally upset his life.

This theory is too pat. It's mainly based on the few police officers who experience emotional problems after a shooting, not the majority who come through it glad to be alive. This theory ignores whatever emotional problems an officer might have had before the event. It also ignores what happens to criminals who kill. It doesn't account for other events surrounding a shooting, events which often have a serious impact upon the shooter's life.

Let's see how this might apply to you, and if you have to worry about the emotional impact of taking a life. First, if you have any moral scruples about defending yourself or your loved ones against a criminal attack, don't get a weapon. Say your prayers and prepare for the slaughter.

FEAR

Secondly, do you know how you react to intense fear? Have you ever thought you were going to die, such as in a traffic accident? If you've ever had an out-of-control gasoline tanker miss you by a few feet while you watched horrified, you may know this. If your car has ever gone into a wild, high-speed skid on an icy road, you'll know what it means to think you may die in the next few seconds. If you've ever been the victim of a violent criminal attack you'll know that fear is normal in such situations.

Some people feel that it's not macho to admit to fear. To feel fear is normal, it's common, and we can go as far as to say that anyone who isn't afraid in some circumstances has something wrong with his emotions.

The aftershock of fear can be severe. It can lead to all of the symptoms of post-shooting trauma. Soldiers who experience these symptoms are diagnosed as having combat fatigue, or combat stress syndrome.

Adding to this is coming face to face with someone who's seriously out to hurt you. Most people don't ever encounter a killer, and the victims of killings don't live long enough to develop the emotional symptoms that facing this sort of hate brings on. Knowing that someone hates you enough to kill can be very upsetting. Being the object of an actual attempt can lead to symptoms.

ATTITUDES

Surviving a violent affray leads to immediate problems. Many are happy to be alive, and rejoice in the victory over the assailant. However, they have to be very discreet about this, as it's considered bad form in our society to adopt such a positive attitude towards violence. People expect us to maintain the hypocrisy that killing was a distasteful necessity which we would have gladly evaded if it had been possible.

If you stand up and say that you're "glad the bastard's dead," people will look at you in a funny way. If you admit that anything positive came out of the experience, such as saving the state the cost of a trial, don't say it in front of the police. If by chance you feel that you enjoyed performing a useful social function, and wouldn't mind doing it again, keep it to yourself.

It's also bad form to be vengeful. We're not supposed to be vindictive, but understanding and forgiving to criminals. There are many who maintain the fiction that Twentieth Century society is civilized. This is why prisons are run for rehabilitation, instead of punishment, these days. We're expected to maintain the veneer of civilization even in the face of very uncivilized criminals. This, too, is hypocrisy.

Don't be hypocritical with yourself. It's all right to feel that you gave the bad guy what he had coming to him. You're not a terrible person for feeling that way. After all, you didn't break into his home to threaten him and his family. You didn't menace him with a weapon to steal his wallet.

THE POLICE

Once the smoke clears, many problems remain. It can be very trying to be faced with a police interrogation immediately after surviving a shoot-out. You won't be treated as a hero. Instead, you'd better expect to be treated like a suspect.

The personalities of the police investigators have a lot to do with the way they treat you. They may be kind and sympathetic, or they may be cold and hard, demanding that you justify yourself and every move you made.

Some police officers resent the citizen who defends himself. This implies that they don't need the police, and some officers will take offense at this. Likewise with public prosecutors. Some believe that police officers should be the only ones allowed weapons, whatever the law actually reads, and they'll make every effort to punish a citizen who shoots another person, even in self-defense.

The other side of the coin is that a police officer who shoots a citizen often has to prove himself to investigating officers from "Internal Affairs," who will conduct a searching inquiry. This is to ensure that the shooting was legal and in line with departmental policy, and to forestall any charges of a cover-up.

Your station in life also will affect the situation. If you live in the affluent part of town, earn a good living, and are well-known as a respectable person, it'll be much easier than if you live on the "wrong side of the tracks." If you're a member of a minority group, you can expect even rougher treatment, even if the officer isn't a bigot.

LONG-TERM EFFECTS

The long-term aftermath of a shooting can be stressful. If your case is one which gets headline treatment, you can expect more harm than good from the publicity. Unfortunately, many journalists feel that firearms should not be in private hands, that the price to be paid in criminal victimization is an acceptable one. If you shoot someone in self-defense, you may be labeled "vigilante," by journalists who either don't know or purposely confuse the difference between self-defense and vigilantism. You might be able to sue some of the more vituperative journalists, but a lawsuit is typically nasty and prolonged, and will often simply get you more negative publicity.

Some friends and acquaintances will react negatively to you because you're now a killer. You'll also find others reacting positively to you because they're violence groupies. You may get very tired of being asked how it felt to kill someone, especially if you've already been asked fifty times.

If the suspect survives and comes to trial, testifying can be an ordeal. Typically, trial dates are set and postponed several times. The anticipation can wear on you. If the suspect or any of his friends threaten you, this won't help either. If the suspect is out on bail, there's a real danger to you, and the need for vigilance will be a burden.

You can expect hostile questioning from the suspect's attorney. If the suspect or his survivors bring a civil suit against you, this can lead to several years of anxiety.

EMOTIONAL SELF-DEFENSE

What can you do about this? Are there ways to avoid the emotional problems connected with defending yourself? The answer is both "yes" and "no." You can't avoid all of it, but you can minimize the impact of the after-effects.

Being honest with yourself is the important first step. If you adopt society's hypocritical attitudes, and try to tell yourself that you are wrong in feeling what you feel, you'll be in for trouble because of the conflict between the two.

Another important step is to realize that people are different. Some react strongly to stress, while others seem to slough it off. Let's be careful here and distinguish very carefully between being genuinely unaffected and faking an uncaring attitude. Be true to yourself and admit which personality type you are. You don't have to tell anyone else.

Start by checking out your attitudes. How do you feel about taking a life if it's justified? If ever you've gone through it, you may already know the "glad to be alive" feeling. Can you be honest with yourself and admit that you can feel good about killing someone, or are you going to succumb to what seems to be society's guilt over the sad event? How do you feel about counter-aggression? Do you feel guilty about doing to him what he tried to do to you? Do you feel guilty because you feel good about it?

Another part of the answer lies in preparing yourself for the aftermath. Do you keep your head under stress? Can you tell a coherent story to the police after coming through a life-and-death confrontation? Are you afraid of the police? Do you cringe when you see a uniform?

Your immediate circle may have a profound effect on how you pull through. If you're the "loner" type, used to making your own decisions and living with them, the opinions of others won't matter as much. If you need other people's attention and approval, you'll be leaning heavily on family and friends after the event. Your family and friends can be supportive, which will help a lot if you need someone on whom to lean. If your family and friends shun or condemn you, it'll be much more difficult.

All of these factors can be important. All of them can help or hinder. It's best to start planning now how you'll handle the emotional aspect of fighting to live. Emotional survival is as important as physical survival.

IF YOU GET SHOT

This is a miserable prospect, but it could happen to you despite your best efforts to make sure that the other guy gets it. Bad luck and human error can hurt you.

The odds of getting shot aren't as bad as they might seem at first. The criminal you face may not know as much about firearms and tactics as you do. He may not have practiced as much, and almost certainly hasn't practiced under adverse conditions. He almost certainly is depending on the intimidation value of his weapon, or he would have shot you already.

If he pulls the trigger, it's not hopeless. Inspector Paul Weston cited almost 50 cases from the records of the New York City Police Department in which the criminal's weapon malfunctioned.[1]

HOW DOES IT FEEL?

Getting shot feels differently to different people. The sensations described by people who have survived gunshot wounds fall into several categories:

1. Pain where the bullet enters.
2. Numbness but no pain.
3. Feels like getting hit with a hammer.
4. Feels like a burning pain.
5. Not much pain at first, then shock, and possibly unconsciousness.

Some state that truly intense pain occurs much later, when recovering from a gunshot wound.

If you get shot, it will be a supreme test of your willpower. You'll have to try to ignore the hurt and still try to put your opponent down. If he's wounded you fatally, you'll surely want to take him with you. If it's not a fatal wound, (don't waste time trying to find out: you'll know soon enough!), keep shooting because his next shot might be the fatal one.

One reassuring fact is that most handgun wounds are not fatal. If you get hit, you have an 80% chance of surviving.

SELF-HELP

After you've put him down you can concentrate on helping yourself. There may be bystanders who can summon help. Meanwhile do what you can to help yourself. You have two problems; bleeding and shock.

A wound that's just oozing blood doesn't mean that you're not bleeding severely. The bleeding may be internal. You can't do much about that. If you can see bleeding, direct pressure will stop it or slow it down. Use a handkerchief if you can, but your bare hand will do if necessary. Don't worry about infecting the wound. If you don't stop the bleeding, you won't live long enough for an infection to develop.

If the injury's in your arm or leg, a tourniquet will work even if you pass out. A tourniquet left on too long can bring gangrene and loss of the limb, but that's better than bleeding to death. If you have to drive yourself to the hospital, you can loosen the tourniquet every fifteen minutes to allow some blood to circulate.

Shock is very dangerous. You can pass out, and if you'd been applying pressure to a wound, you'll lose more blood and deepen the shock. This vicious spiral can kill you quickly.

To fight shock, lie down immediately. Your blood pressure will be low and your brain may not be getting enough blood if you stay upright. Next, take a few deep breaths to make sure you're getting oxygen. Try hard not to relax, and fight any sleepy feeling you may have. Tighten your muscles to raise your blood pressure. Elevate your legs to drive more blood to your brain.

If there's no help on the way, and you can't drive, do something else. You may pass out later, so don't delay. If you start feeling better, this may be merely the deceptive prelude to losing consciousness.

Try to get to a phone. Make sure whoever you get, operator or police, understands that you've been shot and need an ambulance. If you can't phone, break a window. Fire a shot. Do anything to attract attention.

For more information on immediate treatment of gunshot wounds, take a "First Responder" medical course. This is a 40-hour course that gives the basics, but better than the usual watered-down first-aid courses. "First Responder" courses are usually available through a local community or junior college.

NOTES

1. *Combat Shooting For Police,* Paul Weston, Springfield, IL, Charles C. Thomas, 1967, p. 44.

A FINAL WORD

Human life is precious, although some people act as if they don't think so. More specifically, my life is precious to me and yours is precious to you. So are the lives of your family. If someone threatens the lives of you and yours, you have the right to defend them.

Whether you believe in life after death or not, this life on Earth is the only one you've got. We only "go around" once, and whatever happens after the ride is over is another matter. We all want to ride until the last stop, and anyone who tries to push us off the bus before we arrive deserves to have his ticket canceled.